GARDENER'S NIGHTCAP

Persephone Book N° 66
Published by Persephone Books Ltd 2006

First published by
Jonathan Cape in 1938

Reprinted 2008

Endpapers taken from 'Fritillary', a
1936 block-printed linen designed by
Margaret Calkin James
© Elizabeth Argent

Typeset in ITC Baskerville by Keystroke
High Street, Tettenhall, Wolverhampton

Colour by Banbury Litho

Printed and bound by Biddles, King's Lynn

ISBN 978 1 903155 561

Persephone Books Ltd
59 Lamb's Conduit Street
London WC1N 3NB
020 7242 9292

www.persephonebooks.co.uk

GARDENER'S NIGHTCAP

by

MURIEL STUART

✳✳✳✳✳✳✳✳

PERSEPHONE BOOKS
LONDON

Philip Gough.

GARDENER'S NIGHTCAP

by

Muriel Stuart

WITH

DECORATIONS BY

Philip Gough

LONDON · JONATHAN CAPE

To

My Husband

who led me down the Garden Path

NIGHT CAP

And then to bed, to lie with one's face to the uncurtained window, thinking of seed-sowing, and pruning and mulching, and slug hunting, and this year's done, and next year's doings, and all the other garden preoccupations that obtrude themselves so pleasantly before a gardener sleeps.

A GARDEN OF YOUR OWN, WHERE YOU plant and transplant, and are dirty and amused . . .

T. GREY (18*th century*)

GARDENER'S NIGHTCAP

THERE IS AN HOUR JUST BEFORE DARK, when the garden resents interference. Its work, no less than the gardener's, is done. Do not meddle with the garden at that hour. It demands, as all living creatures demand, a time of silence.

At this hour, the labour of day flowering plants is over, and the night flowerers are about to open their shutters. It is the hour of change in the garden, with half its mysterious life stilled, and half awakened.

At this hour is heard the small, rebukeful sound of the wood pigeon, sitting high in the old tree, complaining as though someone had wronged her; the dew has fallen on the grass, the earth is respiring gently, the perfume of day and night are beginning to mingle.

At this hour we should but walk – not chatter, pry nor even praise – like the God who walked in His garden at the cool of day.

In Nature all lovely things pass and come again year after year, but with us they pass, and come not again. We have no second spring. December is all.

TAMARISK AND MANNA

The world has pondered, wondered at, criticized and disbelieved in the miraculous food-'manna' that the exiled Israelites gathered from the ground, 'a small round thing, small as the hoar frost on the ground'.

It has now been found that manna is produced from a variety of the Tamarisk (*Tamarix gallica*), and is still to be found round Mount Sinai, but only after a year of heavy rain, and then not always with certainty.

This strange stuff oozes from the branches and twigs of the Tamarisk, and falls in resin-like beads on to the undergrowth beneath the tree. These beads are incredibly sticky and sweet; 'it was like coriander seed, white; and the taste of it was like wafers made with honey'.

At first the manna is clear and transparent and gum-like; later the substance becomes hard and crystallized, turning an ivory yellow or golden brown like a rough barley sugar.

The manna melts utterly as soon as the sun is upon it, 'when the sun waxed hot it melted', and therefore the Bedouins gather it before sunrise. Science has once more authenticated an old Bible legend.

PIRACY

I know that many people deplore the rifling of the wild, but surely there is a difference between wholesale looting and petty larceny?

The former I have never attempted: the latter I practise whenever possible. I may never see that plant again on my travels. Why should I leave it to be nibbled by a rabbit, or snatched to make a country posy?

It will not be lost, nor does such a small theft ruin the countryside. Most country dwellers are very indifferent to their native plants, and only see them as treasures when they are told that travelling marauders have rifled their walks or hedges.

Besides, who decries the pirates of the Pyrenees, the

stealers of Tibet, the thieving expeditions to Caucasus and Sardinia? Not a soul! Why, such thieves not only steal, but often give the stolen child their own name!

Stealing's stealing. What's theft in Yorkshire is theft in Persia. Our gardens are the receivers of stolen goods, and would be incomparably poorer if strict horticultural honesty had been observed.

Having such words as 'Japonica', 'Chilensis', 'Caucasicum', 'Nepalensis', 'Alpinum' on our garden labels, the unco' honest should do well to keep silent when a native is abducted from the hills of Westmorland.

CLEMATIS TANGUTICA

Lovely Clematis, *C. tangutica*, only by accident did I discover the right position for it! I had hoisted it over a trellis, where it certainly behaved admirably, but one year the old trellis 'gave'; fell down, carrying *tangutica* with it, over an old tree stump of about a foot tall. There, I shamedly admit, it stayed, owing to all sorts of minor disasters, but in the autumn it made a superb recovery over the wrecked trellis and tree trunk, covering it like a little haycock, its lovely suède yellow lanterns sticking up all over it, its leaves spread around it in a soft tangle.

I should never have dared grow *C. tangutica* thus, but I see now, that raised in this way, on a slight eminence, its beauty is more conspicuous than when hugging an arch or fence, for the flowers spring upright from the stem.

NOT SO COLOURED LEAVES

One often buys a tree or shrub for its leaf colour, and they simply refuse to blush!

My Liquidambar, *Rhus Cotinus*, *Cercidiphyllum japonicum*, *Berberis Thunbergii*, and three or four Maples have so far refused to colour at all in the autumn. Yet I have seen them making a perfect furnace in other people's gardens.

But I hear that Maples are often slow to 'turn' in autumn when young, particularly if the soil is too rich. It is better to plant them in poorish soil. I thought mine was poor enough, e.g. barren clay, but evidently it is the wrong kind of poverty.

A LOVELY CLIMBER

Billardiera longiflora is an exquisite evergreen climber, twining gracefully round its support. It is not hardy in any cold district, needing a very warm, sheltered wall in mild localities, but those who have such a wall should hasten to buy it.

Its flowers, greenish yellow fading to purple, are of no particular charm, but the fruit is superb – oblong, and brilliantly blue purple, sometimes an inch long, and seems to cover the whole climber in October. It is quite one of the most beautiful climbers that one can grow.

'LET THE EARTH PUT FORTH...'

The third day of creation must have been a heart-quaking thing. Before hoof or pad or claw appeared to trample, graze or tear, the plant world came forth from the teeming earth. Then the Rose spread her pavilion, the Lily carved her goblet, the Cedar began its solemn spire, the Gentian starred the mountainside with sapphire.

Moss and fern and grass and grain began to colour the dark earth beneath the firmament, beneath day and night. There was nothing then in the world but the waters divided from the clouds, and the earth covered with a mighty covering of flowers.

.   .   .

In our gardens we do not always confine our craziness to paving!

.   .   .

For really gorgeous Marigolds, disbud your plants as you would chrysanthemums. This will turn the homely Marigold into a real queen among flowers.

ROSE VINEGAR

Pluck the rose petals only when they are dry in the sun, and fill with them a bottling jar, and cover with the very best white vinegar, and screw the jar tightly down.

Let the mixture stand in the sun, or in a warm place for seven days, when it should be strained into small bottles, and kept well corked, to be used as a vinegar for salads. It is delicious.

THE MOON AND THE CROPS

It is an old belief amongst natives that the moon affects the crops. When the moon waxes, they say, the sap flows up; when it wanes the sap flows down.

It is wise therefore to plant such crops as potatoes, carrots, beet and other root vegetables when the moon is waning, because the sap flows down, and plant those whose crops are above ground, such as beans, peas, tomatoes, in the first quarter of the new moon, when the sap is rising.

CLOCK FLOWERS

Many flowers get up and go to bed with the clock. Some are early risers, some late. Some stay up long past another's bedtime hour. Childhood's clock flower was the little Scarlet Pimpernel that on a sunny day opens about nine o'clock and closes about three (so it wasn't a very reliable clock for picnics, since we were told that when it closed, rain was about!).

Sisyrinchium refuses to wake before ten o'clock, though the sun may have been out for hours, and closes obstinately about four o'clock. The Evening Primrose rouses itself at about six o'clock, after a night's gaiety, and withers in the morning. The red Flax, *Linum rubrum*, rises at six, and retires at about four.

The South African, *Arcotis grandis*, makes a day of it, for it rises somewhere round seven, and goes to bed at six. *Mirabilis jalapa*, the climber, is a little less lazy than the Evening Primrose, for it wakes at five o'clock in the afternoon, and like hers, its flower is withered early the next morning, while *Ipomœa purpurea* is extremely lazy, for though she rises at dawn, she goes to bed at about ten o'clock!

Many of the dandelion family are extremely lazy, and have earned the name of 'Go-to-bed-at-noon', which they do, sun or shade, having only opened at about ten o'clock.

Anemones may keep shut all day, if it is cold or dull, but normally they open at eight and close at six.

The leaves of some plants are also 'clocks', to a great

extent. The leaves of the Acacia tree hang down in pairs; the Clover leaves fold up, and the Oxalis leaves close down; the beautiful leaves of the Honey Locust (Gleditschia) close themselves in a marvellously exact fashion, each tiny leaflet folded exactly on its twin on the other side of the stalk, so that in the evening, sometimes as early as six o'clock, each leaf stem looks as though it carried leaves on one side only. Sometimes on a dull day the leaves do not open fully at all.

It is an interesting experiment to watch the plants in our own garden, and record their daily waking and sleeping, and the effects on them of sun and cloud.

GARDEN FALLACY

In one's green garden days, one is apt to have the silliest ideas. The bigger the plant, we think, the deeper must be the soil; that anything that begins life in a thumbpot can be contained all its life in a thimble!

We dig a pit for the Michaelmas daisy, and cram an Alpine into a shallow hole. Yet, while quite a lot of large plants spread their roots horizontally, many of the tiny

Alpines demand a depth of soil quite out of proportion to their face value.

Many of these small things which show to the world the merest tuft of cobweb green, or a rosette of silver, have legs ten times as long, which must be allowed to stretch down, down in cool moist soil. It is a crime to possess oneself of plants without knowing how to rear them. We rarely make any other purchase in so casual a way.

CONVERSATION PIECE

'I wish I had your garden. Mine is so new!'

'I wish I had yours. A new garden! Why, it's like a blank book that you mean to fill with verses.'

'If you can write!'

MEADOW SAFFRON

The Meadow Saffron parleys with October, without a stitch on her. For some private impertinence she stands naked, like Susannah before the Elders, and is found faultless. She is wise in her daring. Her leaves are large and plain, and would detract from that glistening beauty which springs slenderly from the dark earth. Long after her death, the leaves unfold to show the place where she lies buried.

The Meadow Saffron resents disturbance, and since her leaves lie brown and withered above her all the winter and spring, light woodland shade, or a clearing in the wild garden should be chosen for her bed.

Her large and faultless crocus cups are tenderest lilac, pure ivory, or a deeper soft rosy purple.

LITTLE SISTERS OF THE WILD

Many of the elegant and aristocrats of the garden have poor relations growing outside in the wild, and very lovely some of these Cinderellas are, though perhaps *Poterium obtusum*, with its spire of rosy beads, might look askance at *Poterium officinalis* (Common Burnet), with its rough heads of purple flowers, which grows in moist meadows. And I doubt whether the magnificent gum Cistus would know *Helianthemum vulgare*, the little yellow rock rose of the downlands, or the hoary rock rose that lives in Wales and the north of England, or the spotted rock rose, though all are comparatively rare.

The lovely midget *Potentilla Beesii*, a tuft of silver leaves and bold yellow-gold flowers, though she herself comes from Tibet, has several wayside cousins. Indeed, one at least is listed in nursery catalogues – *P. tridentata*, who comes back via North America apparently, for *P. tridentata* appears to be our wild Three Toothed Cinquefoil, which is rare, and found, I believe, only in one place.

P. verna, var. nana, is listed as a native, a pale flowered beauty for the moraine: our own *P. verna* (the Spring Cinquefoil) is a small shrubby, yellow flowered plant which inhabits dry English pastures. *P. rupestris,* the large white-flowered Rock Cinquefoil, is as scarce as any Alpine, being found, I believe, in only one county in Wales.

What, I wonder, would *Spiraea bullata* have to say to Meadow Sweet (*Spiraea ulmaria*), rightly known as Queen of the Meadows? Yet anyone can have their spiraeas, if they will leave me Meadow Sweet with its clotted-cream flowers, and dizzy scent which was just beneath one's nose when, as a child, one went meadow wading.

Some of the Cinderellas stand up well to their elder sisters though. *Iris pseudo-acorus* (the yellow Corn Flag) has large beautiful flowers, which she bears reflectively above the standing pool; while the Stinking Iris, for all her horrid name, carries a satchel of brilliant scarlet seeds all the winter, which is more than some of her betters deign to do.

And the yellow Welsh Poppy (*Meconopsis cambrica*), with its slender growth and delicate golden flowers, is a lovely native inhabiting the rocks of Wales and other mountains, while *Glaucium flavum,* the yellow Horned Poppy, growing on the sand by the sea, is handsome enough for any garden, because of its large, glaucous leaves and big golden flowers.

And for airy grace the Campanula family might recognize the Harebell of our heaths and downs, raising her blue minaret in the air from a hairlike stem, and also her rarer, white sister. The Harebell is the child of lore and poetry, Campanulas are not!

Nettle-leaved Bell Flower is certainly a rough fellow, but *C. glomerata,* the clustered bell flower, is pretty enough with its deep blue tubelike flowers in a tapered cup.

Polygala chamaebuxus is a very grand little bush with its beautiful shaped little yellow pea flowers, but the little Milkwort (*Polygala vulgaris*) is also lovely in its way, with its brilliant blue, rosy mauve, or white starlike flowers nestling on the downlands, while brilliant blue *Polygala calcarea* (Chalk Milkwort) has been raised to the peerage in nursery catalogues, and becomes a beautiful little Alpine, a treasure for the rock garden! (Though I believe they stole her from the Maritime Alps!)

We have, of course, native pinks, and heaps of native Saxifrages, including *S. oppositifolia, S. aizoides,* and the two rare native Saxifrages, *S. hicubus,* the yellow Marsh Saxifrage, and *S. cernua,* the drooping bulbous Saxifrage, which sends up solitary white flowers among the Scottish mountains.

Some of these are well worth collecting for the wild garden, for they have the dangerous beauty that evokes memories.

THE WHITE ŒNOTHERAS

There is a distinct charm about these pale Evening Primroses, though they are not often seen, many of them being far more beautiful than the yellow kinds.

Œnothera marginata, for instance, has beautiful frail, sweet-scented flowers, often four inches across. It is a little difficult to establish sometimes.

Œ. speciosa grows some two feet high, and has pale grey-green foliage, and the saucer-shaped flowers are ivory white with centres of creamy green. It is a beautiful plant.

Œ. taraxacifolia is another beauty, with large, glistening flowers and fine-cut foliage.

Œ. trichocalyx is an annual, growing about two feet high, with dark leaves and cup-shaped, pinky white flowers about two inches across, with ivory stamens.

VEGETABLE WAYS

Why do we only train our runner beans upright, and let our marrows wander over the ground like tanks?

Runner beans, in dry seasons at all events, do much better if allowed to ramble about. They get more moisture, and more shade from the earth, and the beans themselves keep far more tender and juicy, and their yield is certainly no smaller than that of their brothers strung up in the hot, dry air.

As to marrows, those who like that somewhat un-interesting vegetable will do far better to grow them like tomatoes – on very strong stakes. The marrows ripen better, and do not rot as they may do on damp ground.

Cut the marrows when they are six inches long, and you have a delicate dish. Of course if you grow your marrows as large as Zeppelins there is no help for you. They must cumber the ground as usual.

I have often wondered how tomatoes would do as ramblers: they would get more earth warmth, and less sun, of course. In some parts of Canada they grow large crops in the fields in this manner.

THE GREEN GARDEN

'Colour!' cries the gardener, forgetting that green is Nature's favourite.

In big old spacious gardens, Time has taken the question out of the foolish gardener's hands. He may plant his geraniums and his asters, but the older, wiser gardeners have planted their yew, their laurel and their cypress, that only the foulest vandal dare destroy. Though I have known people into whose worthless monied hand an old Manor was delivered, who uprooted a four hundred years old yew hedge, thick, black, spicy and wide as death and night, to make room, my God, for stocks and asters!

All this nobility, this ageless beauty, this effort of four hundred summers and as many winters hewn down because 'it kept the sun away'. From what? From a penny packet of seeds that any cat may destroy.

Far too little is made in the modern garden of evergreens. In the craze to cram a garden with colour, it has largely been forgotten that colour needs a background, a contrast. And Nature has laid down the inexorable law that that background shall be green.

So we see many a mad Hampstead Heath Bank Holiday of colour gasping and fretful.

Yet the first duty of a garden is quietude – a place where peace may be fostered, where the eye, wounded by the glare of modern roads and modern houses, may rest upon grey shadow and green shade. But from the noisy street one is so often led into the noisy garden.

It is this pitiful preoccupation with colour that makes the gardener unconcerned with, and blind to the beauty of evergreens. He does not say of a plant, 'What is its form?' but 'What is its colour?' And so too often the garden is a tumble of twisted silks from an overturned workbox.

Plants have none of the regal beauty of form and purity of outline of the evergreens, tree and shrub. Often only staking and tieing allows them any kind of beauty of outline at all. Often the flower spike itself is the only beauty. In shapeliness what flowering plant can compare with the comeliness of *Juniperus communis compressa,* of *Cupressus allumii* and *viridis,* of Rosemary or *Taxus fastigiata* or *Thuya orientalis?*

I will swear that a garden planted only with evergreens would be more beautiful than a garden planted only with flowers. For in November the latter would be a bedragglement of spent flowers, pods and bents and withered leaves – and would remain so for many a month. In the former the garden would hold precisely the same beauty in December as it did in June. It would have retained its form, its colour; it would let no ugly fence or wall gape between its solid ranks.

A man making a garden once said to me, 'What shall I plant?'

'Evergreens!' I said.

'Evergreens? Why evergreens?'

'Just because of that!' I said.

But he thought I was mad, and went out and bought a box of calceolarias!

And because there are many like him, the noble evergreen is left to the gardener who loves green and to the nurseryman who tends the lonely shrubs; and many a legion of Cypress and Laurel and Juniper, and all the host of Cedar, and mountain Pines cry in vain.

Question: What is the first thing the average gardener says when planning a garden?

Answer: 'Herbaceous Border.'

PLEASURE ORCHARDS

I often wonder why our orchards are so purely utilitarian. Of course fruit for commercial purposes must be grown on strictly businesslike lines, but often quite a large piece of land belonging to a private garden is used in this way.

In olden times orchards were also pleasure gardens, both in England and abroad. Arbours, fountains, steps, seats and flowers all played a part in such orchards. And since fruit played an important part in their diet, the fruit could not have suffered under the treatment.

I should not care to see a fountain playing in an apple orchard, but why should not an orchard of full-grown trees be properly turfed, and contain paved paths, and in the centre a pleasant courtyard with a pool and seats? This would save space in the garden proper, and make the orchard a place of beauty as well as of utility.

What could be more heavenly than to walk in such an orchard, to sit by the pool and watch in it the reflection of the still branches, to see the petals dropping on the quiet coloured stone, and on a moonlit night behold the trees in their ghostly bridal white?

A GARDEN ON WHEELS

The saddest thing that can befall a gardener is to become an invalid. He can tend no more the herbaceous border, plant and prune the shrubbery, set and shape the rock garden, nor set a tree against the sky line.

But gardening of some kind there must be for the gardener, however limited. If he can go no more to the garden the garden must come to him.

So take a trolly table and make your garden. Have made a stout shallow wooden tray that will stand in the top tray of the trolly exactly – one made with handles for lifting out, the sides of the tray being deep enough to conceal thumb pots, or a size larger, for henceforth you must garden in miniature.

This garden can be wheeled beside your couch or bed,

the legs can be cut down if the trolly be too high. The lower shelf may be devoted to garden books, catalogues, scissors, and a tiny fork for stirring the earth.

This garden cannot be always at your side. It must be wheeled into the garden for your plants to get light and air; or if your room is upstairs, the tray will be lifted out and placed safely in a sunny spot.

But you will have your gardening hours. You can handle the tiny pots, snip off dead flowers, gently prick the soil, water the little plants, watch that which was a bud yesterday brought to you as a wide-blown flower to-day.

What you fill your garden with depends upon your taste, but it must be in miniature. You cannot have a coster-barrow in your sick room, large plants that you cannot easily tend. It is the handling that counts in gardening.

A collection of small cacti and succulents is a perfect treasure for such a garden, needs extraordinarily little attention, and has a very subtle attraction for a certain type of gardener. Or you can have your rock garden, or a miniature 'Alpine house'. Or again you can grow a collection of dwarf conifers, dwarf willows and other tiny trees, or seedlings from the home woods and abroad.

39

If some of the plants outgrow your pots give them to another gardener, and fill the place with another thumbling.

Here in no small measure you can recapture and retain the garden thrill, grow new plants, adventure and explore, and have at your side your garden on wheels.

DARK LADIES

Fritillary to me spells enchantment – not the arrogant Crown Imperial, but the sombre, dusky Snakesheads, who hide their thoughts in their chequered bells.

It is neither riotous in colour nor prodigious in flower, not obliging in fecundity. It is a mysterious solitary plant, like those women whose charm is for the few but for those few absolute and enduring.

Some of the Fritillaries have thin, delicate leaves, growing upright, close to the stem, such as *F. gracilis* and *F. Drenovskii*; in others the leaves are broader, more lilylike, such as *F. glauco-viridis*; some bear solitary flowers, others two or three to the stem; these flowers contemplate the earth, and only upon raising their heads does one discover the real beauty of Fritillary.

Our own native wild Snakeshead, *F. Meleagris*, the Lazarus Bell of country lore, is one of the most beautiful, but some very lovely ones come from the Balkans and North Africa.

Though the Fritillaries give one the impression of twilight and woodland shadows, they nearly all prefer sun, and the soil that goes with sun – sandy grit. *F. Oranensis*, for instance, from North Africa, needs light sandy soil and full sun. It grows some eight inches high and has beautiful solitary deep purple flowers, chequered with green, and green nectary.

F. Karadaghensis likes the sun too. It is a dwarf species, with strange green bells marked with soft brown. It is rare but hardy and is deeply attractive.

The stems of *F. Graeca* support one or two drooping dusky red-green bells veined outside with green; *F. lanceolata* grows tall, sometimes to two feet, and carries a cluster of green and brown mottled bells. *F. pudica* is brighter than most of the family, dangling soft yellow bells on six-inch stems. *F. pluriflora*, too, has a few brightish pink bells hanging from short leafy stems: pretty plants, though they have not quite the same charm as the duskier Fritillaries.

F. Eggeri has soft tawny cups and grows a little over a

foot high; a rare Persian species needing a very sunny spot – a beautiful creature.

F. Camschatcencis is, I think, one of the most beautiful. Its drooping bells are nearly black – black with a gleam of purple – and pale yellow anthers. *F. citrina* has dusky yellow cups, suffused with green, an interesting looking flower. *F. libanotica* hangs a dark head above its solid glaucous grey leaves.

There is a beautiful Japanese Fritillary which I have not seen – *F. verticillata*, with large ivory flowers, which I am told is very lovely indeed.

And still the chequered English Snakeshead holds its place, with its tessellated, beautifully shaped cups. Unlike the Eastern and African Fritillaries, it likes light shade, and is often grown on the grass of the wild garden.

I haven't found the Fritillaries easy, but then I'm a pretty amateur gardener, but they are supposed to be easy in light, gritty soil, in a sunny spot. But 'easy' is such an elastic word. Probably they *are* quite 'easy' if one knows more about them than I do. But they are worth trying, even if you have to follow the funeral. At least, they are if you like this kind of flower. Either you will say, 'Rather a dull affair', and cast it forth for a clot of colour, or you will reach for the catalogue, and add as many Fritillaries to your bulb list as your purse affords. They should be planted in October, and flower in April or May.

PRESERVING AUTUMN LEAVES

There is a very simple way of keeping their colour in maple, berberis, beech and other glowing leaves that otherwise would fall. Bracken and bramble, too, answer to this treatment.

Get a deep jug, and put into it equal parts of glycerine and water. The mixture should be four inches deep to start with.

Strip the lower part of the stems, and place them in this solution, adding every second day four more inches of the glycerine and water.

When the jug is quite full, the sprays will be ready to face the winter, and should be placed in dry vases.

BETTER GOOSEBERRIES

Gooseberries, more than most fruit, need a great deal of light and air to give good crops. When you prune these bushes, make each bush a hollow cup, by cutting out the centres, leaving, as it were, a stout rim of branches. They fruit far better, and the gooseberries are very much easier to pick.

SINGLE FLOWERS

Roses are beautiful, but they lack personality. They are very pretty women, but no wits.

It is an impertinence of me to speak of roses, and if I can't praise them, I should give them the tribute of silence, but the single roses alone seem to possess individuality.

All double flowers have rather a stupid look, perhaps because they are eyeless. How intelligent the sisyrinchium looks beside the carnation! How quick-witted and alive the anemone seems beside the chrysanthemum, how vital the incomparable Austrian Briar, beside Frau Carl Druschki!

Perhaps the single roses attract me because they remind me of the little dusty roses that straggled in the hedges in the lanes where I was a child. They rebuild the lost country of childhood. They set my feet once more on a lane leading towards a brook, where they grew as best they might, between hawthorns and dogwood, and all the other crowding creatures of the hedge. And in the dry ditch below was the smell of small, pink nettles and ground ivy.

And there I picked the wild small roses. And in the autumn, going home that way, I could still see the hedges where they grew, and beyond them the cattle lying like boulders in the mist; could hear the straw somewhere near stirred by small things, and the gentle thud of sheep going down upon the grass.

By then the wild roses had swelled with small, tight fruit, with all next summer in their satchel.

Grown-ups never realize how close a child is to the earth, how intricate and detailed the earth is to him. Things that to older eyes are but tufts and pleasant tangles, are to him as distinct and individual as the furnishings of a doll's house. He sees the tiny life between the stones, the entrancing growth of very small plants, just as Rossetti, face down amongst the grasses, noted that the wood spurge had 'a cup of three'. We learn on dust, from Socrates, from the field daisy. But only in childhood do we live such lessons.

GARDENER'S APRON

When making a gardening apron, don't make the usual deep pockets in the front. When kneeling, or squatting as all women gardeners seem to do, these bulging pockets may be extremely painful to one's front portion!

Set the pockets well to the sides; you may look like a pack mule, but you'll be far more comfortable. To prevent the apron sagging forward, attach a narrow elastic to the back of the apron sides, which will keep it in place.

.   .   .

The garden, at least, is a world in whose intimate joys and sorrows one is not asked to share. For that is one of the beauties of the plant world. The passing of a flower is so easily replaced, while we can replace neither lost people, nor lost places.

Flowers may plague, vex us for a moment by their refusal to flower, their sudden decline, their unsuspected death, but we think to ourselves we can throw them out, or cut them down, or mulch them, or prune them, or do something of the kind, whereas we can't so easily dispose of those human beings whose lives are linked with ours. But there are always lilies. . . .

. . .

Are you shamed by a clothes line post in your garden? Then on the top of each place a miniature dove cote. Of course there will be no doves, but the birds will perch there, and it will give some kind of apology for a tall, naked post!

PATCHWORK GARDEN

I can never conjure great swathes of flowers, nor trot the unwary guest through a fanfare of Iris or a pride of Lilies.

Mine is no formal garden that reminds one of a transfer

pattern for needlework, no lovely mob of colours: it is a patchwork affair, full of failures and attempts; often ill-placed, and ill-designed – rather like a poem that one is always working on, with which one is never wholly satisfied. It is full of impulses and afterthoughts, a kind of horticultural *esprit d'escalier*.

But after all, the happiest gardener is the one who works to please himself. The garden is his workshop, not his 'Best Parlour'. A wholly tidy, wholly well-filled garden may be a joy in the eye of the beholder, but it holds no lure to the gardener who wishes to advance in garden experiment.

LAVENDER HEAD CUSHIONS

For the deck-chair in the garden, nothing is sweeter than a lavender cushion. Fill a gay cotton case with the lavender, and string it by two tape loops to the head of the chair. It perfumes the hair very sweetly and keeps gnats and midges at bay.

A cushion of mixed herbs may also be made, taking Thyme, Rosemary, Bergamot, Lavender, Balm, Southernwood. For those who like the smell of peppermint, a little Nepeta may be added. These should be dried, and then rubbed very small, in the fingers, and placed in a gay cover. Insects dislike these cushions enormously.

.　　.　　.

Never plant young trees, particularly fruit trees, in pasture; the grass is poisonous to them in a young state, besides depriving them of air.

An area of at least three feet should be left clear round each tree.

NOVEL PLANTING HINT

The following planting method is said to ensure safe planting at all times of the year, particularly evergreens. Fill the hole with boiling water, let it subside, place your plant or shrub or tree on this warm bed, fill in in the usual way, and it will flourish exceedingly.

Sounds risky, yet warm, sterilized earth is an excellent medium.

D

THE FIGURE IN THE GARDEN

THE QUESTION OF FIGURES IN THE garden is a very delicate one.

But unless really beautiful figures can be bought the garden is far better without them, for nothing can give a more jarring note.

Those gnomes with scarlet caps, those brightly painted rabbits and pheasants, the outsize toad, the alarming red cement owl are *not* beautiful, and do not belong to gardens. Why not a doll or a rocking horse?

They are not, surely, meant to deceive? One knows that gnomes and pheasants do not remain perched in odd positions on rocks or amongst roses.

A beautifully designed stone figure is another story.

Stone may well be a natural part of any garden, but it must not startle, any more than boulders startle. It must be so much part of its surroundings that one does not question it. The 'breast of the nymph in the brake' astounds no one.

The loveliest figure I ever saw, the only one I ever bought, was that of a little stone boy. Every aspect of that little statue was beautiful. I did not tell myself then, why it went to my heart so deeply, this little naked boy in white stone. Many times I circled round it, like a somnambulist tranced, and silly as a hen on a chalk line.

And then a veil lifted, and I saw before me Adam as he used to be, Adam of my first garden,[1] who is now learning to be a forester, far away.

It was Adam as he used to look, clambering out of his bath, or sitting sunbathing in Fool's Garden, just a thin naked little boy, with cropped head.

And as I stood, bemused, the spider pounced on me from a little hut, through whose window he had been spying for purchasers, too wily to tempt me while I wavered on the edge of the dream.

He murmured a few words, whispered the price, led me to the hut, and there watched me sign a crazy cheque

[1] *Fool's Garden.*

with pen that trembled as if signing a death warrant.

'Nice little Noode!' was his last remark, astonishing in its simplicity. 'Some ladies like 'em with a bit of skirt on,' he added, allowing himself a little liberty of speech, now that the delicate negotiations were concluded, 'but what I say is, "Give me a noode for out-of-doors. I don't hold with stone petticoats, anyhow".'

This hurried my steps a little, for I could think of no suitable reply to the obvious train of thought. I hastened away, a terrible pain in my pocket, but an 'exaltation' in Venus.

'Nice little Noode!' He pronounced it to rhyme with 'food', which gave it a horrid nakedness.

Yet in one thing he was right. Those stout figures, with skimpy pleated skirt and bead necklace, the clumsy, ill-made faun playing Pan pipes, the rabbit, the gnome, the pheasant, are all garden desecrations.

SOOT

Weathered soot, as a fertilizer, is marvellous. Place fresh soot in open boxes in the shed for a month, and it is then ready to use.

Used dry it is excellent for dusting over plants, as

it keeps away slugs and other enemies. It can be forked lightly into the ground round shrubs and plants, where it acts as a fertilizer, and gives a greater colour richness both to flowers and leaves.

It is extremely good for early vegetables, as it keeps the heat in the soil.

The best way to use the soot dry is to sprinkle it evenly from a tin with a perforated lid.

To use it wet, steep a small bag of soot in a bucket of water, and shake it up and down until the water is black. Or a larger bag can be suspended in the water butt for a couple of days. Whatever the strength, it is quite safe to use. It can then be used in place of liquid manure, and makes, I find, the best fertilizer of all.

. . .

Arisarum proboscidium nearly decided to be an animal! Part its leaves, and you think you have found a litter of new born mice with pygmy elephant trunks. A most intriguing puzzle of a plant, liking moisture and a shady spot.

LONELY WOMEN

A GARDENER COMBINES THE QUALITIES
of a mother and a doctor. Maternal care and tenderness
go out to the plant, and also the careful diagnosis and
ministration of the medical man. Thus the garden
embraces the two noblest professions in the world, for
no garden can long survive unless it is loved, unless it is
tended.

In this the mother takes the larger part, as the mother
does in the lives of children, and I would say to all lonely
women, 'Be a Gardener', for in a garden they will find
full scope for the maternal business of creating, rearing,

watching, loving, tending. In the lives of their plants they will realize in no small measure the pride, problems, fears, joys of a mother, and in their growing children they will find the content of Motherhood.

A 'SILVER GARDEN'

Have you ever, amongst other whims, tried a silver compartment in the rock garden? – Silver-leaved Alpines grouped together amongst boulders?

The effect is an enormous patch of silver green frost that never melts, but remains unalterably silver, even when the patch is full of colour.

The variety in size and shape of the foliage makes the patch a thing of great beauty, and though they never flowered, the carpet would still retain an amazing intricacy of pattern.

Amongst suitable plants for this 'silver garden' are: *Raoulia australis*, like a pelt of brilliantly frosted fur, needing good drainage and gritty soil; *Helichrysum frigidum*, another huddle of silver, demands a pocket of scree mixture. It makes a two-inch bush of silver moss, with delicate white everlasting flowers. It looks as if carved from some delicate substance by a Chinese artist.

The Edelweiss, with woolly silver felted flannel flowers, centred with gold, must be chosen; *Convolvulus incanus* is just silver enough to be included. *Potentilla nitida*, silver cushioned, pink flowered; *Paronychia nivea*, whose tiny bracts are dull silver, are others.

The bulk of the 'garden' can be filled with the saxifrages – the Euaeizoon section, which only ask well-drained loam with a little lime, and many of the Engleria and Kabschia saxifrages, which must have very gritty, well-drained soil. There are magnificent rosettes to be had from both of them.

The Mouse Ear Chickweed, Cerastium, though silver leaved, must on no account be included, or the rest of the silver will be utterly overlaid and suffocated.

MOUNTAIN SPINACH

Atriplix hortensis may be used in place of the ordinary spinach; *A. hortensis rubra*, however, is used as decoration. It grows about three foot tall, and has red leaves, stems and seed vessels in autumn.

It looks very attractive when placed near plants with grey or silver leaves. It should be treated as a half-hardy annual.

THE IVIES

Ivy is not so well known as it deserves to be. The name conjures up the dark dull leaves that covered dull walls, or ambled dustily round shrubs or trees.

But some of the new Ivies are beautiful, and well worth using as decorative climbers. Hedera Gloire de Marengo is very beautiful, its dark ruby stalks bearing beautifully variegated leaves with white margins fading into silver grey, and centred with deep green.

H. colchica variegata has leaves of soft shades of green and lemon; *H. aurea elegantissima* has small, gold variegated leaves. *H. elegantissima* has lovely small leaves tinted with green and pink, and margined with ivory.

These Ivies, though perfectly hardy, do not really care

for a hot, sunny wall, and there is no reason to make room for them there, when they will adorn a duller, colder aspect with more beauty.

An Ivy for the bigger rock garden is *H. minima*, which disdains all support, and grows perfectly erect like a bush, with the tiniest of prettily veined leaves. Another is *H. conglomerata*, which crouches against the stones.

.   .   .

Do you want to grow superb Love-in-the-Mist, that loveliest of all annuals? Then do not scatter the seed in the spot where they are to dwell. Instead treat them like half-hardy annuals. Raise them in small pots, and thin drastically till only the one plant remains in each pot, and then plant it out.

You will not get so many plants, unless you use a great many pots, but each plant will be a superb one, and the flowers magnificent.

THE BEAVERS

Every Iris that has a beard wants full sun. This is its chief desire. It can hardly be kept too dry. These Irises like well-drained soil, containing lime, but chalky ground holds too much moisture for them.

They like bonemeal, and detest manure. They dislike draughty corners or sunless spots. They like a top dressing of old soot.

They should be planted between July and September, the earlier the better: the rhizomes should rest practically on the surface of the soil, so that they can sun-bake. The rhizomes should be planted tip outwards from the clump. Every three years they should be divided.

According to some authorities the Beards like heavy limy clay, and some of the most superb Irises I ever saw outside the Royal Horticultural Hall were grown in deep, heavy loamy clay, with a subsoil of chalk and flint. This rather contradicts the rest of the instructions, but the fact remains. And to confound them further, I am sure there must have been leaf mould in the soil, for the border was in the drift of a line of old beech trees, continually buffeted by a western gale!

If you are a true gardener, you will work with joy in anybody's garden. Flowers are flowers, wherever they grow. Not he who owns the garden most deeply loves the rose – of necessity. Every garden is mine while I am planting.

. . .

How one dislikes the gardener to whom none of one's treasures are new, nothing difficult! One who can tell you glibly the nomenclature, family and origin of every plant he sees (particularly your own pet one, which you had thought would surely be a surprise!)

. . .

The only charge against little blue Lobelia is that she always keeps such vulgar company.

. . .

The curse of a poor gardener is the time he has to wait before acquiring his booty. From a list of perhaps some fifty names, he has to draw an odious black pencil line through perhaps half, three-quarters. That means the loss of a year to him. I know of no more heart-rending business than this job with the pencil. One's garden becomes a kaleidoscope in which plants combine and re-combine to suit one's purse.

WAY OF THE WILD

Have no doubt, have no delusions, a garden is not merely a place of grass and flowers and forms and colour. It bears a potion as dread as Mandragora, a love-cup as fatal as Iseult's. It is a place of continual mating, momentary nuptials, Paphian frolic. The bee is thrust into the flower, the light pollen falls upon the ovary: fertility is carried in haste by the wind to the bride's chamber. And death is in all these cups. It is the way of the wild. And the wild has no pity.

.   .   .

The more we clip the seed vessels, the more ardently does the mother plant labour to bring forth other children. We might learn a lesson from such mothers. Meet opposition and setbacks by putting forth fresh blossoms of courage and energy.

A MEADOW GARDEN

THE GARDEN IS THE NURSERY OF RICH
Cousins, and the wild children of the fields are not at ease
in their company. They are gipsies, tented in a field
corner, or huddled in a windy fastness of the hills. They
would feel alarm in the rich bareness of a garden bed,
and feeling alarm, would probably steal forth on a little
strangling foray of their own!

But if you have a garden that ends imperceptibly in a
meadow, a meadow garden makes a pleasanter frontier than
a fence or hedge, suggesting a link rather than a barrier.

A young tree or so, a bank, a stretch of stony earth,
a pile of flints, stuffed with soil, are all you need, and if

you have space for this wild treasury it will bring the spirit of the open country to the door. For no garden, however beautiful, gives the same sense of contact with the earth, of kinship with the air, of harmony with wind and dew.

Lovely disorder is no tenant for the garden, while it is the lord of the untutored earth. A garden can be untidy; a field never. For every ell of earth is cunningly filled: every patch is stitched; the roots embrace underground and make a mattress that defies the knife. There is none of the sorry aspect of neglect after absence, nor ruin after storm. The peasant weave of the meadow shows no rent, where the embroidered silk of the garden is easily dishevelled.

In making the meadow garden, get as many tussocks from the downs or fields as possible, and set them close to each other, watering well, and filling the spaces between with wild grass seeds. It should be thinned in places to allow such plants as like waste roadside patches to grow happily.

A grassy slope is best, if possible, sloping away from the garden to thinner grass below, and of course there must be a little goat track through it — trodden earth with a few pebbles sunk in it.

Small saplings may be planted here and there: acorns, beech nuts, holly berries can be buried there, tiny sapling ash and silver birch, and seedlings of gorse.

The plants for this meadow garden are numberless. Choose above all the flowers you loved as a child, Wild Toadflax, Betony, Comfry, Rest Harrow, Milfoil, the Campions, Corn Feverfew, yellow Rattle, the Burnets, Ragged-Robin, Rose Bay and Fumitory, yellow Archangel and Lady's Slipper and white Clover. You do not want a well-arranged collection of specimens, you want the freckled meadow in which you lay as a child. Hedge Law and Field Covenant are strict: there strangler meets strangler, and thief engages thief, till both give in and learn to conform to the Hedge Law.

There are certain flowers associated with our childhood that stand out with peculiar clarity and enchantment. For one it is the white Clover, for another the Toadflax, for a third Sweet Mellilot.

Round such flowers, too, hangs a sense of mystery, begotten, perhaps, by something in their surroundings which, when first seen, was associated in the child mind with something mysterious. Perhaps there was something eldritch in the dark hedge near by, or the ditch below was eerie: or something rustled unseen and started in the undergrowth: perhaps the wind moaned suddenly, or a shadow moved across the sun.

Apart from such memories, meadow flowers recall to all of us long hot hours beneath a wide pale sky, the rough embrace of hay, the buzz of bees, the flicker of butter-flies, the picnic eaten by the brook; of holidays, and the smell of bunches of flowers in hot hands.

In such a meadow garden one can recall such hours, plant the flowers that had a stronger, stranger spell for us than any other. We can lie face down in our meadow grass, inside our garden boundary.

Whenever a pod, seedhead or capsule is seen in the fields afar or near home, pluck it, and scatter the seeds thickly in the meadow garden. When a plant is taken, take as much of the surrounding soil as possible round the roots. I have found that if wild plants have a good quantity of their immediate nourishment to start them in their new spot, the further soil is not of great importance.

The charm of such a garden is great. It does not add to our garden labour; the inhabitants grow, and die, and bring forth after their kind, equable, giving no anxiety, and so much quiet pleasure.

INDIVIDUAL ROCK GARDENS

I have often dallied with the idea of small, individual rock gardens of tufa or water-worn stone, set at intervals in paving or in turf. Such gardens would have their advantages. One could journey all round them, and the aspects would be more varied. Each could be built, and filled with the soil suitable to its inhabitants. One could get much nearer the individual plants, and take better care of them, for they would all be within hand's reach.

One such garden might be given over to the Silver Saxifrages: another to Sempervivums: a third might contain only the rarest, choicest Alpines.

Unless one has the money to spend on large, perfectly planned rock gardens, we are often faced with aspect problems that would be solved here, for every 'garden' would have its four aspects.

True, the landscape effect would be missing, but there would be the same interest that one finds in trough gardens, and yet there would be more opportunity for variety than a trough garden can give. It is a pleasant idea to dally with.

WATERING

Watering in the gardener's dictionary may mean anything from a 'sprinkling' to a 'soaking'.

In the Ideal Garden, I suppose, one would not water at all, but few of us have ideal gardens, and drought is common to all.

Constant hoeing is the best way of keeping the moisture in the ground, the powder-like surface preventing it from escaping; overhead spraying of plants on warm nights, particularly of evergreens, which are doubly thirsty creatures, also helps in dry weather.

But if you definitely have to water plants, let it be a 'soaking', not a sprinkling. It is difficult to judge the amount of water given to a plant by means of a hose. One thinks gallons have come through in a few moments, but fill a two-gallon can from a hose, and you will be astonished at the time it takes for the hose to fill it!

It is better to lead the hose to the border, and fill the can from it, so that you can see exactly how much water the plant is receiving. The water must penetrate the soil deeply, or the roots, instead of going down in the quest for water, will try to come up to reach the surface water, and will consequently feel the effects of the hot soil and sun, disastrously.

THE PROBLEM BORDER

Many gardens have a problem border, one perhaps too narrow to be called herbaceous, too wide to be merely an edging; too small for a shrubbery, or too shady for a rock garden. Nearly every garden seems to suffer from such a border . . . an odd border that calls for special treatment.

The answer is the rock border, a garden for those larger rock plants which endanger the smaller alpines, and while not herbaceous in character, are in themselves extremely attractive.

Very little stone is needed for this border; a boulder or two, just to show the uninitiated that it *is* a rock garden, are quite enough, if the border verges on turf or on crazy paving. If it is one leading from the gate, or flanking a gravel path it should have a neat edging of irregular stones, between which tufting plants can be set.

You have no idea what a delightful and original collection of the larger rock plants can be grown here, which, if you have only a smaller type of rock garden, you may have to forego. Such plants are quite happy in ordinary soil, and need no cosseting; they make lovely patches of colour, and provide additional interest to any garden.

If the border is in the open it is best to keep the taller plants to the centre, leaving the sides for the smaller ones, so that it is well designed whichever way you approach.

If it happens to be beneath a wall, plant one or two wall-hugging shrubs as a pleasant background. Right in front of the border you can plant such pretty things as Corydalis, the homely but comely Lungwort (*Pulmonaria*) and tufts of Thrift, dwarf Campanulas, and Stachys.

Old-fashioned favourites, such as Candytuft, yellow Alyssum, and Arabis do well here. The perennial Candytuft (Iberis Snowflake), a foot high, has exceptionally large flowers, while *Arabis grandiflora rosea* has dainty shell-pink blossoms. The tall *Alyssum rostratum* with hoary leaves and brilliant yellow flowers is little grown, though very attractive here.

But don't make a formal edging to this border. Have, for instance, a tuft of Corydalis, then a couple of small boulders over which the Thyme may creep; then a patch of Ajuga, and so on. Otherwise you will lose the character of the rock border.

This border is by far the best place for the taller Stonecrops, which should be better known. *Sedum spectabile*, the Japanese Stonecrop, 18 inches, is extremely decorative with its plump, fleshy grey leaves and flat heads of old rose flowers which the butterflies love. Another Stonecrop, *Sedum populifolium*, makes a compact bush like a small tree, and its white flowers are sweetly scented. *S. purpurescens*, with dark leaves and violet flowers, and *S. spectabile* are particularly useful as they flower well into the autumn.

Both the Flax and the Toadflax are lovely in this Alpine border; the yellow Flax, a small evergreen bush, is profuse with lemon flowers, while the well-known blue variety looks beautiful beside *Sedum spectabile*. The Toadflax, which as children we all loved, needs no describing, but there is a new variety (Canon Went), 18 inches, with exquisite pink flowers.

Other desirable plants for the border are the larger Alpine Pinks, Lithospermum Antennaria, the dwarf Potentillas, the smaller Hypericums, and Rock Rose or Cistus. Many Campanulas may be included, such as the dark-belled *C. pulla,* and *C. rotundifolia,* and for an edging, *C. pusilla* and *pusilla alba.*

For early flowering the big Megasea Saxifrages are extremely handsome. They bloom in March, and their large, plump spikes of waxen, firm pink flowers are not only splendid in the open, but most effective in vases.

The position of the Alpine border does not matter, except that if it faces north you will have to modify your choice of flowers. But in every case keep strictly to plants that are rock plants in character.

.   .   .

What compensations there are for the untouched heart. When the weir has quieted itself into a lake, when the mountain ceases to tremble at the still, small voice, when one is preoccupied with things, not people, when beloved pursuits are not despoiled by beloved invaders, when we have turned to the things belonging to our peace, how tranquilly we can take trowel in hand, without being interrupted by those uneasy thoughts that assail us when we begin thinking of people, rather than things, and go unscathed about our garden business.

71

A LATE ALPINE

Genista dalmatica is particularly valuable as it flowers in July, always a dull month in the rock garden.

A sunny crevice should be chosen for it, where it will cover itself with golden flowers. It is quite a spreader, creeping over the wall space which it hugs closely, though making a hummock of only a few inches in height.

NAME THIS FLOWER

How sweetly some of the flower names sound! Not those that tell us that Mr. Wilson or Mr. Smith stood sponsor at their christening, but the wild, sweet names by which the country knows them.

A great deal of imagination has gone to the making of these names, with the pinch of truth that all true poetry contains.

It must have taken a poet to call the Elecampane, with its rough, stout leaves, and dull yellow flowers, Ploughman's Spikenard. Some hind, with whom Poetry walked as he followed the plough, bestowed beauty upon a country simple, for a volatile oil and a bitter resin are extracted from its roots, known in France as Vin d'Aubnée, and used for lung complaints.

The name Doronicum hails from Arabia, though what Arab could have associated the Great Leopard's Bane with leopards?

Rough Marsh Bedstraw conjures up admirably the wild marshy tangle where it grows. It is also known as Bode

Straw, or Praying Straw, on whose whorls peasants tell their Aves. Slender Hare's Ear, the country name for Bupleurum, has to the imaginative somewhat the look of a hare's ear in the grass, while Stinking Goose Foot is all that its name implies, the leaves being rounded, with triangular base, exuding a horrible fishy smell.

A clash of opinions over the merits of the yellow Dead Nettle must have caused its various names, Weasel's Snout, and Archangel, neither of which seems entirely appropriate. A legend has it that the plant was named after St. Michael who came to earth to explain the invaluable medicinal uses of nettles!

Broom Rape well describes that parasite strangler, which seizes on the roots of Broom, Furse, Clover and Ivy. It is a queer, sensual looking plant with thick club stems, adorned with sticky reddish bracts and dull ochre pink flowers, well deserving its brutal name.

Loosestrife is known variously as Creeping Jenny and Herb Twopence. It is undoubtedly a creeper of the most impudent kind, and its round leaves arranged in pairs accounts for its other name, so called by someone returning home with empty pockets, perhaps.

Water Soldier describes perfectly a curious plant that grows in watery ditches. Its upright leaves protect like a sentry box, an inner sheath containing one white, round-petalled flower. A strange habit of the Water Soldier is to come to the surface to show the flower, afterwards sinking back, sentry box and all, into the mud.

Sauce Alone, a country name for the wild garlic, may have been named by someone who detested the breath of onions. As Poor Man's Treacle it seems to have a touch of cynicism.

A rare woodlander is Herb Paris belonging to the Trillium family, known as True Lovers' Knot. It bears on the stem top four large pointed leaves, from the centre of which springs a spidery shaped green flower speckled with gold. Some lover waiting for his mistress in the tree shadow must have named it so from the four ribbon-like leaves. He must have waited and wandered for some time, head bent, for Paris is not easily found!

A delightful name for a tiny, modest plant that lurks in wet and marshy places is Water Blinks. I should like to meet the namer of Water Blinks. It is an affectionate, puppy-like name.

The Colt's Foot is enchantingly named Son-before-Father, because its flowers always appear before the leaves. Its name Colt's Foot refers to the large hoof-shaped leaves, the resemblance being probably

75

strengthened by the shaggy flower stems. Naming Valerian was a matter of taste. Some one who liked it on his wall called it Good Neighbour; some one who did not, called it Kiss-Me-Quick, a very hasty and dutiful embrace being indicated on account of its strong rank smell. Other country people called it more succinctly Phy, and Faugh!

The mysterious Fritillary Meleagris, with its checkering of ashen rose and green and black, has no name more suitable for its strange and sinister appearance, than Lazarus's Bell. Some village Beaudelaire must have seen in it the bell worn by lepers, that warned men of their terrible approach. Yet Fritillary that followed the feet of the Romans was esteemed by Gerard for the 'bosomes of the beautifull'.

One rarely considers when calling flowers by their homely names what a marvellous amount of imagination and observation went to their making, what simplicity of vision, what unlettered but vital sense of poetical comparison.

Would you or I be able to name the flower so aptly, so poetically? Should we see a spikenard in Elecampane, a leper's bell in Fritillary, a good neighbour in Valerian, a Creeping Jenny in Lysimachia? I doubt it. We are troubled with Latin and Greek, with the outer wisdom rather than the inner wit.

It was left to the wandering hind, the dreaming shepherd, the loitering wench, the busy herb woman to give them such names. In their daily work, in their toil among the furrows, in the evening saunter down the lane, they looked upon their native plants as part of their lives, as easily named as their children. And in their poetic awareness they chose the fitting name, beside which our precise Latin has a dull, visionless sound.

ROSE OIL

Collect some fresh dry rose petals, and scatter a little salt at the bottom of a dry glass jar. On the salt lay a layer of rose petals; on the layer of petals put a circle of cotton wool which has been saturated with lucca oil.

Continue until the jar is full, pressing lightly down the last layer. Cover the top of the jar with parchment and fasten firmly down.

Set it in strong sunlight for three weeks. Then strain the contents through a piece of muslin, squeezing every drop of oil out. A delicious rose perfume is the result, and should be stored in glass bottles.

YELLOW ROSES

Although I am not particularly fond of yellow flowers, I find yellow roses always the most attractive of their tribe.

Mermaid, the yellow climbing rose, is one of the most beautiful, and is, I confess, one of the few roses I have ever bought. Having bought it and planted it in an impossible situation, I moved it, in sheer shame, to the sunny side of a lych gate. There, outraged in some way, the whole length of her died, and I cut it down to within a foot of the ground, never expecting to see her again!

But she needed this major operation, apparently, for she made great to-do, and began to climb most busily up the lych gate, spreading along the roof. There she finally burst forth into a galaxy of pure sulphur yellow single flowers, five inches across, with fringed amber eyes, set among varnished bronze leaves, keeping up the display from June to the last days of November.

Another yellow climber is Hugonis, with very small, dainty leaves, and delicious small butter-coloured dog roses. A very sweet and delicate climber, its only fault being that its flowering season, though early, is rather short.

Christine is a really beautiful rich yellow rose which makes a small bush of sturdy and continuous blooms. McGreedy's Yellow is a most beautifully shaped pale soft bloom; Mabel Morse is deeper yellow, while Golden Gleam has particularly beautiful buds.

Perhaps the queen of all is Phyllis Gold, very large, very pure in tint, deeply scented and long flowering. To me her only fault is that she is double!

I do not like ramblers of any kind, but if I had to grow a rambler I should choose Emily Gray. The leaves are very decorative and the manes of yellow flowers never seem to fade.

Both Golden Rambler and Phyllis Bride are touched with pinkish red – an unforgivable sin, I think, in a yellow rose.

.   .   .

The beautiful fruits of Barberries, Pyracanthus and other shrubs which give such gay warm colours at the turn of the year, are often spoiled by the birds.

Extract of quassia is the answer. Sprinkle the bushes with this solution, diluted, and the greediest bird will think twice before pecking at a berry that looks so luscious, yet has the taste of Dead Sea Fruit!

WINDOW GARDEN

A tiny garden for somebody who has no garden at all can be made with very little trouble, and lasting delight. I saw one such on the window-sill in a gloomy London flat.

A piece of felt had been fitted to the bottom of a green glazed shallow oval dish. Then the dish was filled with small pieces of rock and pebbles, no bigger than plums. In between the stones were placed tiny pieces of Stonecrop, one or two very small ferns; small bulbs, and seeds of Alpine Cress, a trail of ivy-leaved Toadflax and other easy and obliging midgets.

The felt was kept continually moist, and it was extraordinary how the roots found their way to the damp felt, and thrived thereon.

HOLLY BEADS

Holly beads make decorative necklaces. String the berries on stout thread, and let them hang up to dry in a warm room. Occasionally work the berries lightly up and down, so that they shall not stick to the thread.

When the berries have dried they look like very deep red, rough coral. Give them a final polish by rubbing them lightly with cotton wool damped with brilliantine.

NURSERY LORE

Nurserymen take it for granted that, when we order a plant, we know all about it. If we order a Liriodendron, for the beautiful yellow-green flowers, so glowingly described in the catalogue, he concludes we know that the Tulip Tree does not flower till well in its twenties; that Catalpa, the Indian bean, is also a laggard, and produces blooms only at maturity.

The ignorant gardener does not know that plants listed

as 'five foot', means that eventually, under certain conditions, they may attain that size. They often leave the nursery as pygmies, and may not flower for years.

The ignorant gardener orders a five-foot conifer. It is not for the nurseryman to tell him that big conifers, and indeed many other shrubs, particularly evergreens, resent being moved at that height and age, and need expert care to keep them alive.

There are certain questions that the ignorant gardener should ask his nurseryman.

1 What height will the plant be on its arrival?
2 How long should it take to reach the height mentioned in the list?
3 When may it be expected to flower?
4 Is it 'tender', e.g. susceptible to (a) frost, (b) cold winds, (c) drought?
5 What aspect suits it best?
6 Is it a plant that dislikes being moved?

I shall not soon forget the cynical remark of an old gardener, in a nursery garden, when I was ordering a Weeping Birch. The trees, I was told, were seven and six and ten shillings each.

'And what is the difference?' I asked.

'Well,' he answered, 'sometimes folks is lucky, and

sometimes they ain't. If they orders a ten-shilling tree, and we has only a seven-and-six size, they gets the seven-and-sixpenny, and if they orders a seven-and-sixpenny, and we only has ten-bob ones, then they gets the ten-bob size.'

Since that day I have always ordered the second size, trusting that I shall be one of the 'lucky' folk!

COLOUR

Gertrude Jekyll's dictum that a garden must be a garden picture has been misconstrued by many gardeners. In her picture that great gardener included with colour, form and interest, but her disciples too often pick the colours from Joseph's coat, and ignore both cut and material.

A garden should be more than a mass of flowers. It should be a community of individually interesting plants. Colour is not all. We only grow as gardeners when we desire form as well as colour. Plants are not mere units of colour.

In Japan some of the most beautiful of their gardens

are pure examples of form. One famous 'garden' consists solely of a few perfectly placed pieces of stone. One has only to examine their miniature trees to see that form plays a far more important part in the humblest Japanese gardener's art than in ours.

Tyranny of colour leads us from adventure. To get these swathes of colour we are apt to use flowers that are suitable to our purpose, often those of the commonest and most hackneyed varieties.

Bemused with colour the gardener neglects form and interest. A new delphinium draws a crowd. A little new tree or rock plant scarcely stops a few loiterers.

WINTER TREE COLOURING

The bark of many trees and shrubs adds magically to their grace, though few people buy them for this beauty.

Betula Nigra peels its ash-grey coat to disclose broken shades of coral and ash-ochre. *B. Ermanii* has an exquisite ivory trunk, and orange-red branches; *B. lentas'* bark looks like black marble.

The stems of the 'Violet Willow' are almost violet

in colour, covered with grape-like bloom, most beautiful on a winter's day. There are other Willows with brilliant orange, yellow or crimson wands.

Amongst the Chinese Maples is one whose bark is a maze of dark silver, with soft beetroot tracings; another has a lovely stem marbled in moss-agate colours. *Acer Henryi* has stems suffused with blue.

The Japanese Maple, *A. rufinerve*, possesses a mother-of-pearl bark of pale green and silver. The Liquidambar has a heavily corrugated grey-brown bark, which is very effective. The bark of *Arbutus Menziesii* is smooth and the colour of cinnamon, smooth as satin, peeling away like flakes of tissue paper.

Amongst the dogwoods, *Cornus alba atrosanguinea* has blood-red stems; *C. stolonifera* has bright yellow bark; *Prunus serrula tibetica*, the Ornamental Cherry, has glorious polished red chestnut bark.

MOVING EVERGREENS

A good idea when evergreens have to be moved from one garden to another is to tie the ball of earth in a piece of sacking, stuffing the sacking as tightly as possible with fine earth, tightly tied to the stem. On arrival, immerse the plant, still in its sacking, in water, if at all dry, and plant the evergreen in its coat of sacking. This will soon rot away; the new roots push through it quite easily.

All evergreens, however short a distance they are to be moved, should be moved with a large ball of earth attached to the roots, so that there is practically no root disturbance. They should be placed in holes already thoroughly moistened, and thoroughly firmed in.

DON'T THROTTLE THEM

There comes a time when the herbaceous border is put into corsets: a stout string attached to a stout stick gives them the look of careless Victorian dowagers.

No plant was ever meant to grow in this way. Pea sticks should be placed round these dowagers in their earlier youth, so that the plant has grace to grow more or less after its own fashion. When the plant is mature, the sticks will not show, and the whole effect will be that of a large vase of graceful flowers.

Also, this freedom gives the whole plant more light and air, and the chance to develop all its flower heads properly.

VARIEGATED PLANTS

VARIEGATION GIVES A VERY SATIS-
factory sense of unchanging colour-mass in the garden.
It supplies a mass of quiet colour which no flower can
give, since few flowers have so long a life as their
foliage, and are not always certain in their blooming.

Variegation is found in tree, shrub or plant, and can be
used most effectively in the garden, its quiet harmony
adding both to flower and evergreen.

Amongst the trees, perhaps the Maples give some of
the most beautiful leaf variegations. *Acer Negundo
variegatum* has green, white and silver leaves, some of
the younger foliage being entirely ivory, or tinged with
rose, the green of the leaf being at no time considerable.
It makes a gay contrast to dark evergreens.

A. platanoides Drummondii is one of the finest of
variegated silver trees: *A. Negundo californicum aureum*
has beautiful golden variegated leaves. The slender
A. palmatum roseo-marginatum has pale green leaves,
margined with coral.

Amongst the Elms is *Ulmus nitens variegata,* a small

tree, with mottled silvery grey and white leaves, and
U. viminalis aurea, a slow grower, whose leaves, while
not strictly variegated, are prettily suffused with soft
yellow.

The Beech, *Fagus sylvaticus tricolor*, has beautiful
burnished coppery leaves tipped with pink and white.
Fraxinus pennsylvanica variegata, a very decorative tree,
has silvery leaves, edged and mottled with rich ivory.

Among the shrubs *Sambucus nigra pulverulenta* is an
elder with leaves variegated white and edged with pink;
the variegated Privet I mention because it *is* variegated,
but a ghastly little shrub, I think!

Fuchsia macrostemma variegata has pleasantly variegated foliage, and one of the Wiegelias, *Diervilla florida
variegata* has silver variegated leaves.

A really attractive Cotoneaster is *C. horizontalis variegata*. In autumn the silvery leaves tinged with red look
most effective amongst its berries.

The Dogwoods, too, have variegation in the family.
Cornus mas aurea elegantissima has very striking foliage,
the graceful leaves being variegated with yellow and
tinted and edged with rose. *C. Alba Spathii* has very
pretty golden variegation.

The variegated varieties of Euonymus are very much

more attractive than the dull green associated with that rough old shrub, and there are some nice dwarfs – *E. radicans* (Silver Gem), whose leaves are faintly bordered with pink: and *E. radicans variegata*, both delightful compact edgers.

Pittosporum tenuifolium, a rather tender, and very beautiful shrub, with soft green, holly-like leaves on black twigs, enormously decorative for vases, has a variegated variety, *P. tenuifolium* (Silver Queen), the leaves of which are softly suffused with silver.

There are several prettily variegated hollies, both gold and silver, which look very well in association with darker leaved shrubs.

Among the hardy evergreen St. John's Worts is found lovely *Hypericum Moserianum tricolor*, suitable for the rock garden, not quite so hardy as the rest, with lovely golden flowers and leaf variegation of pink and white.

Amongst the climbers there is a most beautiful Ivy, *Hedera canariensis variegata* (Gloire de Marengo), whose leaves, dark at the centre, merge into silver, which in turn merges into an ivory edge. The stems of this Ivy are a rich deep beetroot colour, while *H. elegantissima* has small, nicely shaped leaves, tinted with rose and edged with milky white.

The climbing Honeysuckle, *Lonicera jap. aureo-reticulata*, has leaves netted with bright yellow.

The ornamental Vine, *Vitis Henryana*, a very handsome Chinese climber, covers its leaves with a network of silver, pink and green, which is most attractive.

Actinidia Kolomikta has most beautiful foliage, half ivory fading into an edge of deep, delicate shell pink, and its white flowers are faintly scented.

The little, excellent 'ground coverer' Periwinkle, *Vinca major elegantissima*, bears its blue flowers amongst brightly variegated golden leaves.

Amongst plants are the beautiful variegated Thymes, such as *Thymus cit. fol. aureus*, and Silver Queen, which make such picturesque borderers; one of the herbaceous Veronicas, *V. gentianoides variegata*, is a very nice, compact bush with cream green foliage and spikes of mauve-blue flowers, excellent for the taller edging.

Ajuga, that excellent carpeter, has a prettily silver variegated variety, *A. reptans variegata*; while *Pulmonaria saccharata picta*, a homely but attractive plant, suitable for the rougher rock garden, has blue, and broad handsomely variegated leaves.

THE WILLOWS

The members of this very decorative family vary from ample trees to the smallest creeping shrubs. They come from many districts in Europe and Asia, including China, the Himalayas, Siberia, the Alps, and also North America.

Amongst them are found some of the most graceful trees in the world, and nearly all of them have attractive catkins, and many of them great brilliance of bark.

By the waters of Babylon, the desolate women of Israel hang their harps upon the Willow; on the famous blue and white Willow pattern china, a Chinese Willow takes its place in picture and rhyme. From the Willow the cricket bat is made, and the humble basket. The tree from which the sportsman's bat is formed is always a female tree!

Amongst the most beautiful of the larger varieties are *Salix daphnoides*, splendidly decorative for the large garden. Its winter stems are the colour of plums, having too, the plum's bloom, and handsome catkins in the spring.

The Golden Willow (*S. vitellina*) is a weeper with slender, pendulous branches of ochre yellow, looking in early spring a fountain of pale gold. It can be kept a low shrub if planted as a border tree, by cutting it down every spring, so that the young stems may become even more brilliant in colour.

A Willow prized for its magnificent branch colouring is *S. vitellina britzensis*, whose wands are rich orange-scarlet.

One of the loveliest is *S. pendulina*, rivalling *S. babylonica* in grace, and hardier, for the *babylonica* is inclined to be tender in cold gardens. Its branches are very long and slender, its foliage narrow.

These Weeping Willows have a tremulous beauty lacking in other weepers, and are of the highest decorative value for gardens.

Our own country supplies the Palm Willow, with its silky soft ashen catkins. This is the Willow that is sold in bunches, about Easter time. *S. alba argentea* is a beautiful native semi-weeper, with silvery leaves, and *S. viminalis* is prized for the best kind of basket work.

Wilson's Chinese Willow, *S. magnifica*, is not, in spite of its name, so attractive as the smaller-leaved Willows; its foliage is very large, broad and blue-green, resembling the laurel leaf.

S. rosmarinifolia is a smaller compact shrub, about ten

foot, with very delicate, grasslike leaves, a beautiful little tree.

Amongst the smaller Willows are some very attractive bush forms, suitable for the smaller garden, and very dwarf Alpine species.

S. Bockii, from China, makes a three-foot, pretty shrub, its chief attraction being its striking catkins which appear in late September. *S. purpurea*, the Purple Willow, is extremely graceful, hovering between a bush and a small tree, with elegant, purple-red branches.

There is a beautiful small weeping standard form of *S. repens argentea*, with very small grey silver leaves, a good choice for the smaller garden. The native *S. lanata* (the Woolly Willow) is also admirable for limited space, making an upright two-foot bush, with white downy leaves and bright yellow gold catkins.

Amongst the dwarfs of the tribe are some of the loveliest little things for the rock garden. One of the gems is *S. repens*, a perfect 'tree' of a few inches high, its tiny branches laden in spring with powdery gold catkins among the minute leaves.

S. herbacea, the tiniest of all Willows, though it does not look in the least like a Willow, is a native Alpine, with the very smallest, round glossy leaves, soon making a substantial hummock. *S. reticulata* is another very small affair of some four inches.

Willow cuttings strike extremely easily, even those of the Alpine varieties.

RIPENING TOMATOES

There are several ways of ripening tomatoes. One is to pick the fruit as soon as they show any sign of colour (or even before, if the yield is heavy, and you want to relieve the weight of the trusses), and store them in a drawer in the dark. This applies particularly to the late fruits, that in a dull summer have not had time to ripen.

Another way is to place the fruit that is changing colour in a sunny window in rows, turning them now and again.

After the end of September, frost may ruin the remains of the crop, and a good third idea is to cut the whole plant off at the root, and hang them upside down in an airy shed or room.

The gardener who loves Roses, Sweet Peas and Mignonette is apt to deride the gardener who is interested in the curious, while the gardener who prefers form to colour is inclined to belittle the lover of the Rose.

But the garden world embraces all. To each his own delight. Though we are but foster mothers we have the right to choose our nurslings.

Had Blue Lobelia different associations, another purpose, and nicer friends it would be a pattern for all borderers, it is so small and trim and compact, and evenly coloured, everything that a borderer should be.

.   .   .

'Riot of Colour' is a garden cliché.

'PRIZE BLOOMS'

Do the ecstatic whispers, the gleaming trophy, the gilt stamped card mean anything to the prize-winners of the Royal Horticultural Society? By prize-winners I mean, of course, not the grower, but the plant!

95

There is really something almost stupifying about the tremendous mass of prize blooms exhibited at these shows, as if the flowers themselves were bursting with the pride of their magnificence, communicating it to the vibrant atmosphere about them.

Even the small but precious pot containing a solitary 'new' flower, has its own peculiar atmosphere of triumph. It is known that plants have heart-beats. Why shouldn't they beat in triumph?

Foolish idea? Maybe. But how very little we know of the strange, secret hidden life of the plant world.

THE LURE OF THE LITTLE

ONE USUALLY CONNECTS MINIATURE gardens with sinks or troughs, but it is possible to have a delightful miniature garden without either.

The garden of which I speak is a natural garden, not an 'artificial baby one'.

The idea first occurred to me when planning a new garden, on a large table top.

A miniature garden in the open may provide a 'garden within a garden'.

The disadvantage of a trough or sink is that its shape and size are predetermined: the boundary is rigid. In planning such a garden in the garden itself, one can vary size, shape and boundary. It can be enclosed with a dwarf hedge, or with a tiny wattle fence, plaited from small osiers: it can have a gate, and winding paths, and its pond, its dove cote, its seat, its terrace.

But beware an awful snare – that of artificial decoration; avoid the pseudo Japanese bridge, the coloured china figure, the bit of mirror for a pool; the shells for stones.

In envisaging such a garden, the gardener must view everything through the wrong end of the telescope. All must be in proportion, but the size may be anything reasonably dwarf.

It is delightful to experiment with such things, for some of the loveliest plants are very small.

Such a garden should be placed in a position by itself, near a pool, or round a sundial, leaving, of course, space between the sundial and the confines of the 'garden'. It may, if desired, be raised on a low bed, walled with stone, and this last is perhaps the best position.

The shape may be anything to suit the gardener's taste, providing it is a harmonious form in itself, the outline formal or irregular. Experiment alone will teach the gardener here. As to size, about six feet by three feet six inches is a good average.

A very attractive outline may be completed by enclosing the garden in a low bank, surmounted by a pygmy 'wattle' fence, or one made of clipped dwarf shrubs. *Euonymus radicans variegata* is ideal for this purpose.

Inside may be a lawn, a shrubbery, borders, garden pool; any garden plan, in short, carried out on a dwarf scale.

For the lawn camomile is good, for it can be 'mown' and kept close and neat: or very fine turf from seed is an alternative.

Trees must be no more than a foot high, and for these probably the dwarf conifers are best. There are many to be had, mostly with names almost as long as themselves. Amongst the Cupressus are:

C. obtusa nana, a very ancient looking affair, very slow, a dark green pyramid. *C. obtusa pygmaea,* which makes a real tree with a flat top.

Salix repens, a dwarf Willow, with golden catkins, and *Pinus benvronensis,* the pygmy Scotch pine, are other treasures for such a garden.

Other shrubs and plants that may be effectively used as trees are *Thymus carnosus,* which forms a poplar-like little bush; *T. citriodorus aureus,* a variegated little six-inch bush; and Veronica Hectorii, the golden whipcord variety.

For use as shrubs there is a very large variety. Some of the very tiny amongst the conifers make mounds only a few inches high.

Pernettya Tasmanica makes tiny humps of thyme-like leaves, white flowers and large red fruit.

Euonymus radicans Kewensis, a curious, slowly creeping evergreen with marbled leaves: *Bruckenthalia spiculifolia,* a heath-like little shrub rarely attaining more than eight inches in height, with rosy pink heather-like flowers, are suitable.

The dwarf, shrubby Pentstemons also make delightful flowering shrubs, and the very dwarf Rhododendrons, the last needing lime-free soil. One of the Daphnes *cneorum*; the prostrate Willows, *Salix pygmaea,* a gnarled miniature; *S. retusa; S. reticulata* and *S. herbacea* make perfect little 'shrubs', so does *Polygala chamaebuxus,* with its boxlike leaves and rich coppery yellow flowers. Many other Alpine plants may take the place of shrubs.

The miniature grasses, *Festuca glauca* and *F. pumila,* are also very useful and attractive.

Small paths of crazy paving may be used very effectively, leading to a small pool, or seat, or sundial.

The flowers for this garden must be very neat and small in proportion to the shrubs and trees: no plant with very large flowers should be used, or the border effect will be lost.

The tiny Irises, *I. lacustris,* brilliant blue and gold: *I. cristata,* pale blue and orange; *I. ruthenica,* brilliant violet, are all lovely here; they are best planted by themselves in small beds.

The 'herbaceous' border will be, of course, a suitable size for the rest of the garden. Four inches is a good average width. In this may be planted such things as *Thymus serp. minus*, a very dwarf, close grower; *Veronica saxatilis*, neat, semi-shrub, three inches high, with big, sapphire blue flowers; *Sisyrinchium augustifolium*, six inches, whose thin spearlike leaves and China blue star flowers will make an effective 'tall' plant; such Saxifrages as *S. Irvingii*, close and neat, with delicate, nearly stemless rose flowers; *S. Faldonside*, with flowers of the purest primrose; and many other of the rosette-forming Saxifrages.

Raoulia australis makes a patch of prostrate silver fur; Phlox May Snow, a vivid green mound, covered with milk-white stemless flowers; Globularia, has button heads of lavender blue; *Geranium Pylzowianum*, sturdy and pleasant with its ferny leaves and rich magenta flowers.

Dianthus versicolor, four inches, with flowers whose colours change from white to bright rose; *D. neglectus*, whose rosy flower are black-eyed; *Campanula pusilla*, and *p. alba*, both making large mounds, covered with tiny bells: the dwarf Calceolaria, *C. polyrrhiza*, with enchanting 'slippers' dangling on short slender stems; the

Arenarias, the little onion, *Allium cyaneum*, looking rather like a tiny Agapanthus with its pale blue flowers may go here too, and the dwarf daisies. There are, of course, innumerable other small plants suitable for such a border.

Thumb pots, containing seedlings from orange or grape fruit pips, may be stood upon a small terrace.

Small rose borders may be made with *Rosa Rouletti*, the smallest rose in the world, making a six inch bush covered with tiny double pink roses.

Other features of such a garden may be a pergola, or a little well made from very small pieces of walling stone. A beautiful formal pool can be made from the cream-coloured stone bricks from a child's brick-box, lightly cemented together, and placed upon a cement bed. Twelve inches long by eight inches wide is a good average size.

The planning and planting of such a garden is thrilling, but work it out to scale before you start, or you will find that your herbaceous border dwarfs your trees, or your pool is too small for the surrounding lawn.

ROSETTE PLANTS FOR THE ROCK GARDEN

Plants in which the leaves are arranged in the form of a rosette are extremely varied in size, and most decorative for the rock garden. Rosette plants are shapely, compact, often beautifully coloured or silvered, and they fill the places allotted to them perfectly.

Many of them make large mounds of rosettes, forming a kind of beautiful mosaic; some of them hug flat wall faces, stitching the rock with patches of embroidery; some like to stretch themselves out on crazy paving, while others nestle among cool stones. They give, I think, more alpine character to the rock garden than any other kind of plant.

The flowers that spring from these rosettes are usually in plumes or posies, and are sometimes the last kind of flower that one expects to rise from those compact leaf tufts.

Saxifraga lingulata Alberti, for instance, has neat, beautifully silvered rosettes, but it throws a large ten-inch plume of clustered white flowers. *Saxifraga Myra* covers its small rosettes with large, almost stemless, cherry red flowers.

From the Saxifraga family come some of the most lovely of all rosettes – soft grey green cushions, tiny dark leaves, or magnificently frosted and encrusted rosettes. They are absolutely indispensable for the rock garden or the scree. The big crinkled rosette of *Ramondia pyrenaica* produces short-stemmed, beautiful lilac flowers with yellow centres. It likes to sit firmly in a northern crevice.

Little *Sedum farinosum* also likes walling, but prefers the sun, or is quite happy in crazy paving. It makes a posy of tightly packed faintly pink flowers – one of the prettiest of the Stonecrops.

Some of the most surprising flowers come from the Sempervivum or House-leek family. They look so solidly sculptured, so complete in themselves, that one is apt to regard them merely as rosettes, though very beautiful ones.

But suddenly a rosette heaves a bit, and raises a tall shaggy leg bearing on the top a head of starry flowers, faintly resembling the Colt's-foot. There is something extraordinarily attractive about Sempervivum flowers, and many of them are beautifully coloured. One would never guess that such legs could hoist themselves from such demure, woolly rosettes as *Sempervivum arach-noideum*, but it has lovely terra-cotta and gold flowers.

A rare and beautiful plant allied to Ramondia is *Haberlea virginalis*, with a green rosette from which pure white flowers droop gracefully, like small Gloxinias. Haberlea also demands a cool northern crevice in the rock garden.

The Lewisias need all the water you can give them in the summer, and hate a drop in the winter; they want to face south, and be dry, yet never in the least thirsty, and the soil bed perfectly drained. From their fleshy rosettes spring most exquisite flowers.

Oxalis enneaphylla is a lovely little plant for well-drained leafmould and peat and the shadow of a rock. Among its silver-blue loose rosettes nestle large, pearly, sweetly scented flowers.

An attractive Stonecrop of a definitely rosette type is *S. pilosum*, with soft downy green rosettes and heads of tiny shell-pink flowers, extremely taking. This Sedum is biennial, but it seeds freely, and is quite easy to raise.

WATERING ALPINES

In Japan, Alpines are watered with ice cold water, a proceeding that makes the Western gardener catch his breath as if he, too were under that icy spray.

But when one considers that Alpines are under snow for many months of the year, and revel in the snow water that penetrates their roots when the snows begin to melt, this method seems more sensible than dosing them with our luke warm rain water, which is beloved of plants of rainy regions.

DECORATIVE TOMATOES

A novelty for the salad bowl is the 'fancy' tomato. These small-fruiting tomatoes look like plums, pears, cherries or currants according to variety.

The little yellow pear-shaped tomato is particularly attractive, and so is the currant-shaped red.

They have the authentic tomato flavour, and should be placed whole amongst the other ingredients of the salad.

VERBASCUM BROUSSA

The old fashioned yellow Verbascum (Mullein) was a comely plant, but the new varieties must make it feel rather a poor relation. Cotswold Queen has beautiful large pale crushed strawberry flowers; Cotswold Gem has soft buff flowers with purple eye. Miss Willmott is regal, and white, and very tall. Pink Domino is pink with deeper red eye. But the king of the family is Broussa, eight foot of magnificence, completely smothered in cotton wool, through which push rich yellow flowers.

THE COMELY KITCHEN GARDEN

Why divorce the Kitchen Garden from the Flower Garden? The former, which supplies us with succulent fruit, crisp saladings, rich vegetables, spicy herbs, is usually hidden away as if we were ashamed of it. Yet it should be the Pride of the Garden. How often do our steps urge us stealthily from the contemplation of the luxurious lily to the peach that waits us on the wall further on, or the raspberry cane that is as eager as a cow to be milked?

The kitchen garden is as comely, as pleasant, as interesting as the herbaceous border, whose only beauties are scent and colour. For my part, being carnally minded, I consider a ripe peach more beautiful than six delphiniums. It has superb colour, a comely shape, its texture is thrilling, its perfume magnificent; its taste is heaven on earth.

The cabbage has a bloom that few perennials give; the delicate green pea plants, with their ivory flowers and their slender tendrils clutching the fine branches have a beauty that the sweet pea misses — those long, hard waxen pods full of round, delicious peas! The painted fruit of the strawberry is worth the bright flower of the Potentilla every time!

I think it mean to hustle the poor old kitchen garden behind a hedge like a dustbin or a privy, while we batten on her liberal stores and plunder the rosy fruit, pull the waxy carrot, behead the lettuce, and comfort ourselves with apples.

The herbaceous border satisfies two senses only – those of smell and sight: the kitchen garden gratifies sight, smell, touch and taste.

The kitchen garden deserves a prouder place. The rows of peas, beetroot, carrots, lettuces and the like, the lines of well-confined raspberries, and walls trained with lacquered fruit have a severe and harmonious beauty. In my kitchen garden I grow pleasant clumps of annuals. It is bordered with lemon thyme and sisyrinchium, and parsley (everyone grows too much parsley for their needs) makes nice clumps there, with chives and pinks.

Flowers that are picked for the house are good companions for vegetables that are picked for the kitchen.

My kitchen garden is hidden by no decorous hedge, nor modest trellis. It melts into the garden proper, and has its double pride of its beauty and its utility.

GOOD KING HENRY

Its Latin name being *Chenopodium Bonus-Henricus*, it saves time to speak of him in English! Particularly as he is a native.

Good King Henry is quite a good substitute for asparagus, by covering the new shoots every year to blanch them, and should be ready for eating by the middle of April.

Plant the seed in rows fifteen inches apart, in rich, deep soil, and thin out to about twelve inches. The leaves can be eaten like spinach, though the flavour is not so delicate as the proper kind. Still it is a useful plant that can be eaten bud and leaf!

.   .   .

Nicandra, the Apple of Peru is a neglected annual, yet a very deserving one.

It grows tall, about four foot, making a nice bush, with light blue flowers rather like mallows, and very decorative lantern pods. *N. violacea* has the added attraction of a bluish tinge to the stalks and hairs of the leaves.

The seeds should be sown in a sunny border in late April.

RAG BAG MANURE

In some parts of the country snippets of cloth and other material are considered excellent manure. I met an old farmer once, who had three or four women cutting these snips from all manner of ancient garments. Sackfuls of this are dug into the ground in the same way as stable manure in the autumn, and apparently make a grand feeder.

It is I suppose an amateur adaptation of shoddy, the waste from woollen and carpet mills, which is largely used, and which becomes humus when rotted.

These snippets of wool and cloth were used on clayey land, where it breaks up the clay and renders it much more friable.

The real shoddy should not be used by amateur gardeners, unless they are sure of what they are handling. Foreign shoddy is unsterilized, and therefore dangerous.

COROKIA COTONEASTER

A little tree for those who like the quality of strangeness. It has stiff, shiny black, very slender tangled branches. Its leaves in winter are beautifully silvered beneath, and in the spring the new leaves, in shape like tiny fish-hooks, show shades of soft green and bronze, and here and there a brilliant scarlet leaf.

It is curious how close to the earth the majority of early spring flowers grow; the Aconite, the Celandine, the Crocus, the Violet, the Primrose, the Squill, the Snowdrop.

As the year advances, flowers seem to grow taller and bolder, till midsummer finds the borders full of six foot giants!

FLOWER TONICS

One charm of growing Alpines is that they are clean growing creatures. Although I know that 'dust returns to dust', and grass passes back through animal bodies to grass, etc. etc., I have an aversion from animal manures. Whatever they say about stable manure I prefer the 'grass' that has never been anything else but grass.

The primal manure was vegetable, for the plant world flourished before the animal world appeared to defile it.

I cannot, with any complacency eat lettuces that have been tonicked with 'slops', nor carrots and beetroots, nor any crop that has fattened upon cesspool contents, that have been quickened or enlarged by sewage. Horse, cow and fowl manure are not so repulsive, but human excrement is disgusting.

If by the use of such manures one gets finer crops and larger flowers, then give me the lesser ones which have grown in their own soil enriched and fortified by their stems and foliage, or by clean vegetable manures.

The garden teems with manure, from the dead pods of lupins to the despised chickweed, from the cabbage stalk to the leaves of oak and beach and other trees. Every leaf that falls to the ground falls for the purpose of enriching the soil upon which it falls, though it may enrich its own race only, as surely that was intended by Nature.

I do not like flowers that batten on blood and bone. I feel that the physicking of our gardens is overdone. We are always drenching and drugging it, or forcing it. Nothing is left to Nature, and Nature retires, with her strong natural forces, and leaves us to our pills and tonics.

Horticulturally I am probably a fool, and because I will only use hops, or leaf mould, or peat — all vegetable manures, simple herbal remedies — I may be the loser, but at least I shall not have my brother's blood crying to me from the ground!

That is why I love growing Alpines: they ask for such clean food – sand, limestone, leafmould, peat, cool stones.

No maggotty manure, no evil-smelling offal, no dried blood.

And I believe that if we used more vegetable and less animal manure, particularly for the things we eat, it would be to our own well being.

THE MEXICAN TIGER FLOWER

Whoever sees Tigridia in all its glory will never let his garden lose them.

They are rarely mentioned, and not widely grown, possibly because that itch for 'the riot of colour' rejects a flower whose colour is so fleeting. But 'better fifty years of Europe . . .'

Though Tigridia is ephemeral, each flower lasting but a day, its colours are the most magnificent in the garden world.

It is an immense six-petalled flower, having three large slightly pointed petals, and three much smaller ones, halberd shaped, set symmetrically and perfectly between them. From the centre, which is clear and smooth, rises the long, graceful pistil; the outer petals curving slightly back, form the centre into an open cup. The flowers appear in a swathe from long, montbretia-like leaves.

T. var. canariensis has large deep yellow flowers, the cup six inches across, and smaller petals thickly blotched with pure carmine. It flowers in early July.

T. var. lilacea, a little later, has brilliant rose-carmine flowers, the blotches being white. *T. grandiflora* has brilliant nasturtium red petals, the inner sides of the cup, and smaller petals heavily tigered with old gold. *T. pav. grandiflora alba* has ivory petals, cup and halberds heavily spotted with deep carmine. These are the most striking varieties.

Although these superb flowers have the look of orchids, making one feel that the hothouse is their only home, they are quite hardy. I find they do well in a position facing east, in rich soil of loam, leaf-mould and a little sand; the flowers do not wilt so easily as in a Southern aspect.

In lighter soil I do not find that they do so well, though most authorities advise sand and full sun. They certainly like shelter from cold winds, and this is best given by planting them near protecting shrubs.

The bulbs should be planted in late March, six inches

apart, and three inches deep in a handful of sand. It is better to lift them in cold localities, when the foliage has died down, though in warmer districts they may be left in the ground if winter protection is given.

To think that these flowers grow wild in Mexico – if for that reason alone, a place worth visiting!

MAY LILY

A delightful little woodlander is the 'May Lily', *Maianthemum convallaria*. It has glossy light green heart-shaped leaves, and short spires of white, spiraea-like flowers. It makes an excellent carpeter in half shade, or light woodland, or under shrubs, provided the soil is cool and moist.

It spreads rapidly, and the flowers are four to six inches in height, flowering in May.

A HUNDRED GARDENS

Walking one day in a new garden suburb, I wandered down a road of a hundred houses, and being curious to

see what manner of plants were beloved of the owners,
I made a list. It runs roughly as follows:

In 95 gardens: geraniums

In 60   ,,   lobelia

In 90   ,,   white candytuft

In 10   ,,   calceolarias

In 5   ,,   begonias

In 40   ,,   asters

In 20   ,,   snapdragons

In 16   ,,   roses

In 14   ,,   pansies

In 2   ,,   a small tree

In 1   ,,   a pink spiraea

In 10   ,,   canterbury bells

In 80   ,,   privet

In 3   ,,   c. macrocarpa

In 30   ,,   aubrietia

It just shows you! . . .

FRAGRANT SHRUBS FOR THE GARDEN

The names that float immediately through one's mind in thinking of fragrance, are Honeysuckle, Jasmin, Magnolia, and Lilac, but there are many other shrubs whose fragrance, persistent or fugitive, opulent or delicate, aromatic or sweet, make them unrivalled garden company.

Some put forth their enticement in the last days of winter, others at mid-summer, and others in mid-spring. It is possible to have fragrance of some kind in the garden, all the year round.

The sweetest of the winter flowering, sweet-smelling shrubs is *Chimonanthus fragrans*, the Chinese Winter Sweet. Its parchment-coloured flowers faintly touched with dim purple and powerfully fragrant of honeysuckle, appear upon its leafless branches in December and January.

Another is the Chinese Witch Hazel, *Hamamelis*

mollis, whose yellow flowers have a 'rich Eastern' smell. *H. vernalis*, too, has a rich scent in its small reddish flowers.

In February *Daphne Mezereum* shows its very fragrant red-purple flowers, before the leaves, and a little later *Vibernum Carlesii*, with flat clusters of waxen rosy buds opens into white lilac-like flowers, intensely and exquisitely perfumed. Its brother, *V. fragrans*, earlier to bloom, has the same cold sweet smell.

One of the finest of all the barberries, *B. japonica Bealei*, has wands of chrome-yellow flowers from February to April, and a scent very like the lily of the valley – a magnificent shrub from every point of view. The humbler barberry, *Mahonia Aquifolium*, has yellow mimosa flowers in March, which have a fresh, sweet scent. It is evergreen, and grows where many another plant would refuse.

Corylopsis spicata lures the late air of March with the hint of cowslips. It makes a most beautiful, shapely shrub, and before the leaves appear, is covered from head to foot in a shower of pale primrose-coloured flowers. When in full swing, Corylopsis is perhaps the loveliest of all early shrubs.

The tree heath, *Erica arborea*, appears at much the

same time. Among the finest of fronds the white bells, faintly but deliciously scented, are beloved of the hungry early bees.

Some time in April another Daphne makes its presence known by the stealing perfume of its pale rosy flowers. *D. cneorum,* and the evergreen, beautifully flowered *Osmanthus Delavayi,* very sweetly scented, is on its heels.

The scent of the Allspice, *Calycanthus floridus,* pervades the whole plant, as its name suggests, with heavy aromatic scent. It is not a very attractive shrub, but planted in an inconspicuous place, it makes the air rich with perfume in May.

In June the Philadelphus 'Mock Orange' brings its almost overpowering scent into the garden. *P. hybridus* Avalanche has amazing blossoming powers, as well as powerful scent in its large white flowers. *P. Virginal* is a beautiful, richly scented double white; *P.* Belle Etoile has very large ivory flowers, flushed with purple at the petals' base, and deeply perfumed.

A shrub with a very sweet, delicate scent, which few people seem to grow, is the yellow currant, *Ribes aureum,* which has smooth and soft leaves, prettier than the rest of the family – a tubular jasmin shaped flower.

This Ribes makes a bush of some ten feet, and flowers in June.

The old Buddle Bush, *Buddleia variabilis*, which flowers through July, August, and early September, has no need of perfume, with its magnificent trusses of brilliant violet flowers with a tiny vermilion-orange eye. Yet it has a warm, heavy spicy scent, very powerful in the sun. A much rarer, but attractive kind, *B. Fallowiana alba* has richly scented white flowers.

The evergreen Cistus family are noted for the rich spicy aroma of their foliage, the Gum Cistus, *C. ladaniferus* being the most heavily scented, for from this Cistus comes the famous labdanum used in perfumery. Apart from its strong rich perfume, *C. ladaniferus* has an exquisite large white silky flower, with deep carmine patches at the base of the petals, and fringed with gold stamens.

Choisya ternata, the evergreen Mexican Orange Blossom, often begins to flower quite early in the year, but is at its best in May. Its masses of starry white flowers have the intoxicating, bitter-sweet orange-blossom smell.

There is no need to mention the world 'Lilac' for it is perhaps one of the earliest perfumers that one remembers.

Its great fault is that it is such a clumsy bush at all times except just when it is in flower.

The yellow tree Lupin, which flowers in July and August has a very sweet, strong honeyed scent.

A handsome August shrub is *Clethra alnifolia*, the Sweet Pepper Bush of America. Its cylinders of large white, narrow belled flowers have a very delicious smell, and the shrub grows usually to about six to eight feet.

The evergreens, Rosemary and Juniper and *Thuya occidentalis* have strong resinous scents, and the Box its own strong, curranty smell.

FROST AND SUN

The danger of frost is not so disastrous as the after sun. It is not the frost alone that kills the plant, but the heat of the sun, which falling on the frozen leaves practically bursts the veins. A sunny morning after a sharp frost is the most deadly combination. The only way to save a victim is to syringe it heavily with ice-cold water and throw newspapers over it. This particularly applies to a southern border, where the greatest heat of the sun will be felt.

WHY DOES YOUR PATH WIND?

In China no path leading to the door is ever straight, because evil spirits, oddly enough, can only haunt on a straight line. The more winding your path, the safer you are from the devil. I wish this applied to those devils of dogs!

THE THORN APPLE

The queen of this family is the gorgeous ten-foot *Brugmansia Suaveolens*, often known by its old Arabic name Datura, a cool greenhouse plant. It has beautiful smooth, almost tree-like stems, and enormous trumpet-like flowers of purest white, sweetly fragrant.

So substantial and solid are their flowers, that to hold the trumpet (10 inches long, and a foot round at the mouth!) in one's hand gives the impression of holding a large roll of tightly folded paper.

The plants, when grown in tubs, may be placed out of doors in the sun.

The annual Daturas, however, are well worth growing. They make tall, handsome plants, with very large single or double trumpet flowers, white red or pink, very beautiful in shape, and far too rarely grown.

The seeds are best planted four or five to a pot, and raised in a warm greenhouse. Pot them again in three inch pots, and plant out in a warm spot in late June, in rich soil.

.   .   .

Foresworn for ever be the little square lawn, and the little centre bed, and the ribbon of path. Be adventurous, even in the front garden.

.   .   .

Some decency of clothing, some measure of food and drink must be observed by the poor but ardent gardener. I never envied anything in Eden, but the privacy that made no offence of nakedness. So many an illustrious name, many an imperial form goes by a sad pageant of elimination into the Dream Garden that all gardeners possess, which is so much more spacious than their own.

Only by some magic, by denial, by skilful comparison of prices, by eggs for supper, and other shifts that only the poor gardener knows, some of these treasures are saved from the dream garden of 'Next Year'.

THE BABY MICHAELMAS

The dwarf Michaelmas daisies were evolved, I read somewhere, for the graves of British soldiers in France. Since the names of the dead must not be hidden, and an autumn flowering plant was wanted, this little daisy was eventually produced for this purpose.

It is a splendid autumn dwarf, perfectly easy, and a most prodigious bloomer. Growing from six to ten inches high, these little asters make delightful borderers, and also effective pin-cushion bedders. I have seen them in rock gardens, but they are out of place there, though they are very attractive in small beds let into paving.

TREES FOR THE SMALL GARDEN

A GARDEN WITHOUT TREES IS ONLY an allotment. Even the smallest garden can support at least one tree, providing it is chosen with regard to the space one can afford for it.

And one must find out first the maximum size to which the tree will grow. It is disheartening to receive mere saplings from the nursery, which in a few years will cover a great many yards of space and air.

A small weeping Willow, which looks but a rod of slender branches, will in a few years make a tree of very considerable girth as regards branch room, and would completely cover a small lawn.

People with small gardens have the idea that trees will deprive them of flower space. But the small lightly foliaged trees do them no harm. Many flowers grow well in light shade.

All garden trees must take their proper place, and this is far more important in town or suburban gardens. In the country trees grow beyond the garden gate, or in the fields beyond, giving that indispensable green background that all gardens need.

But where bricks and tiles are the background, trees are essential. Nothing is more barren, more sordid than those long lines of naked fences, over which ramblers alone crawl, those fences which begin and end in houses.

For the suburban front garden, the use of trees is both effective and economical. So small a space can hope for little beauty in floral display, and the choice is often too inevitably the cheapest and commonest of bedding out plants. These plants solve only the problem of a fleeting season, and from October onwards such gardens have nothing to please the eye save the forlorn privet hedge which does such stout duty in this type of garden.

Trees in the front garden not only give dignity and beauty: they help to hide the opposite row of houses. Fortunately many suburban architects have become tree conscious, but they cannot dictate to the owners of private gardens.

If only gardeners recognized more fully that a front garden needs be dignified and neat the whole year round! Trees and paving can so easily solve the problem of the gardener who aspires to have an orderly garden before his house.

There is a large variety of trees suitable for the smaller garden, and some for the smallest garden.

Among the flowering Apricots, Almonds, Plums, Cherries, and Crabs, are trees to suit every small garden. The Crab, *Pyrus floribunda atrosanguinea* is one of the most exquisite of small trees, low and horizontally branched, wreathed with brilliant rosy crimson flowers.

Amongst the flowering Cherries, *Prunus Sieboldii*, a small tree of slow growth, clustered with pink flowers, or the upright *Lannesiana erecta*, which grows like a small Lombardy poplar and has beautiful large pale pink flowers. The well-known Almond needs no recommendation.

Other suitable trees for restricted space are: the new Chinese Mountain Ash, *Pyrus Vilmorinii*, a lovely tree, the rosy fruits turning to pearly white tinged with rose, and the very elegant and graceful *Pyrus Folgneri*, which colours well in the autumn.

The Honey Locust, Gleditschia, has the most beautiful, delicately cut foliage of any tree, the leaves turning custard yellow in autumn. *G. elegantissima* is the best variety for a small garden, being beautiful in its pyramidal shape, and rarely seen.

Cydonia vulgaris, the 'common Quince', is another

fine little tree, with beautiful pale white-pink flowers and spicy yellow fruit.

The Judas tree, *Cercis siliquastrum*, literally smothered in rose pea flowers, and *Cornus alba variegata*, whose leaves are variegated with silver, are other very suitable trees, while the double Thorns, crimson, pink or white (a great improvement on the old May tree), and a large number of the extremely beautiful Maples, particularly *Acer brilliantissima*, the spiny leaves touched with coral, and *A. trifidum*, whose early foliage is brilliant red, are all delightful for the smaller garden.

As specimens for lawn planting there are several small 'weepers', such as the 'Weeping Aspen', with attractive purple-grey catkins in very early spring, *Fraxinus excelsior aurea pendula*, the 'Golden Bark Weeping Ash', the 'weeping Purple Beech', and most beautiful of all, the weeping Silver Birches, preferably *Betula verrucosa pendula Youngii*, and *B. verrucosa dalecartica*, the Swedish Birch, both very beautiful weepers.

Some of these small trees are apt to send out side-shoots low down, which give them a shrubby appearance. To maintain a clean central stem, the side shoots should be cut off as they appear.

THE MAIDENHAIR TREE

Ginkgo biloba is placed botanically between the ferns and the conifers. It is a link with the prehistoric times, for its imprint has been found in fossil beds.

It is like no other tree, its beautiful leaves being like some enormous Maidenhair fern, and its fruit like the golden plum.

It is an ideal tree for a small garden, for it grows so slowly, and it does not object to the proximity of towns. Its bed should be warm, rich loam.

It moves well, and keeps its brilliant green through the driest summer, the leaves turning to rich gold in the autumn. The whole tree, seen from a distance, has a most ethereal and delicate air.

SWEET SULTANS

Most annuals respond amply to more generous treatment than they usually get. Sweet Sultan is one. Give it a warm spot, and mix a little bonemeal, a little hop manure and a little mortar or lime rubble with the garden soil, and you will be rewarded with really magnificent flowers.

GOOD COMPOSTS

For Rock Plants:

> One part hop manure, two parts oak-leaf mould, two parts beech mould. Use as top dressing.

For Rhododendrons:

> One part hop manure, one-and-a-half parts fibrous peat. Use as top dressing.

THE WILD COMES BACK

An ownerless garden always wears that neglected look which only comes to places that have once been cultivated. The wild never wears that look, for in the wild are no weeds. The dandelion is on speaking terms with the sorrel; sister grass and brother clover have no sense of being intruders or aliens. The earth bears with equal pride the briar and the nettle. The bee's favour knows no distinction.

Each plant grows where it will, as it can. None are forbidden blow, if blow they may. The harebell on her airy stem is not more regarded than the groundsel with her ragged hair.

But in the garden there is no democracy. There are two classes in the garden – plants and weeds. One class is named, cherished, pampered, honoured: the other class is torn up, cast out, burned, poisoned. They are weeds. They dare set no foot in the Pavilion of Queens. Their purple is not royal, and all their bars are sinister.

Yet plants that are kings in the wild are pariahs in the garden, while the runagates of foreign mountains are lords of the border.

But leave that garden for a while, and by stealth, in silence, slowly, implacably, the wild comes back and takes revenge for its outcasting. Weeds strangle, jostle, choke the forsaken nobles who have become delicate and helpless after much tending. Nettle puts out his harsh tongue; dock pitches his tent; up come the bird weed and the couch grass, the thistle, the burdock; the chickweed with her terrible fecundity, the groundsel in its battalions.

And there is civil war and no quarter, until the wild takes its own again.

CRYSTAL GRASSES

The field grasses have pleasant heads of flowers, but when picked and arranged in vases, lose their delicate pollen colours, and become a little drab and unhappy looking.

To make them sparkle in a dull corner, play the following little trick on them.

Dissolve a few pennyworth of alum crystals in a wide-necked jar of very hot water, adding enough alum until it ceases to dissolve. Then put the grass heads a few at a time into the jar, and let them soak in the solution for twelve minutes. The water must be kept hot all the time.

Then draw them out carefully and put them into a vase – rather narrow-necked ones will look the nicest for grasses.

When the grass has dried, the grass heads will have the appearance of being covered with tiny crystals, which sparkle brilliantly.

THE IDEAL GARDEN

How i should dislike to own a
ready made garden! Of course I admire magnificent
gardens, old or new, but I should not care to own one –
as a garden.

I should regard it as I regard period furniture, and old
Masters, with awe and respect, not possible of alteration
or improvement; mine, perhaps, but only mine as a
guardian of a work of art. It is already designed, static,
perfect. I might be proud of possessing such a work of
art, but as a gardener I should find it dull.

Give me the rough pasture, the derelict area, the place
that might have been a garden once. For a settled and
superb garden gives the imagination no play. A far
finer hand and clearer eye and keener vision than mine
have shaped it and moulded it, have set its perfect
boundaries, its dark trees, its pleasaunces.

I should not wish nor dare to alter it. But in that rough
patch of untilled field I can conjure up, dispel, blend and
dissolve the vision of a thousand gardens.

It will of course never be one half so beautiful as the dream, but it will be a workshop, a nursery, a playground; the place of a hundred disenchantments and a hundred joys of fruition.

Such a garden would be mine, as no other could be, though it will show so plainly the blunders of its maker, that at no time can I survey it, and say, like God, that it is good. God Himself worked such a garden from the waters under the earth.

As I shall have planted everything that grows there, I shall watch the sapling grow taller and straighter against the bright sky, the Alpines pass and repass. I shall stitch and unpick my sampler.

No, I do not envy the possessor of an old and beautiful garden, so long as I may walk in it.

But to walk in a garden is not to work in it. And work is the first, last, best delight of gardening.

Taming a garden is an exciting thing. Give me a garden that shall play virgin to me.

.   .   .

A plant much neglected in gardens is *Gentiana asclepiada*, the Willow Gentian. It is doubly valuable as its flowering period lasts from August right into the latest Autumn. It has not the exotic beauty of *G. Farreri* or *G. Macaulayi*, but it has a handsome look, nevertheless.

Its tall wands bear deep purple-blue flowers all along the stems, and it gives a touch of colour in a shady spot.

The white variety, *G. asc. alba*, has even more beauty.

AUTUMN PAEONY

The fruits of *Paeonia Cambessedesii* are more beautiful than its flowers. In autumn, bursting widely open to reveal a rich violet lining, the seed pods contain polished black and scarlet berries. These decorative pods make a lovely patch of colour in the autumn border.

A LATE SHRUB

November will often find *Osmanthus aquifolium purpureus* in full bloom. It is a dense, compact, slow growing shrub with rich purple foliage in the earlier part of the summer. Then later on the delicate sprays are covered with tiny white, fragrant flowers tucked along the branches. It is a very useful and decorative ever-green for the shrubbery.

SHRUBS WITH UNUSUAL BERRIES

A beautifully berried shrub is one of the loveliest things in the garden. Red is the popular colour for berries in Nature, but some of the more exclusive shrubs exhibit more subtle, less obvious tints.

Sea Buckthorn (*Hippophae rhamnoides*), for instance, has delicious round orange translucent berries disliked by birds, and *H. salicifolia*, very rare, has pale trans-parent yellow berries like half-sucked acid drops.

Callicarpa japonica has round berries of pale pastel amethyst which persist on the bare branches like mauve wooden beads – a unique berry.

The climber, *Celastrus scandens*, has yellow fruits which burst wide open to show flaming tomato-coloured seeds.

Billardiera longiflora, another climber, has the most brilliant deep blue, bean-shaped berries drooping from its evergreen leaves.

Clerodendron Fargesii has large round fruit which turn from China blue to a brilliant sapphire, resting in a deep red calyx. In September Clerodendron is exquisitely beautiful.

Pyrus Vilmorinii is a small tree whose clusters of waxen berries turn to pearl flushed with pale rose. The fruit of *Pyrus hupehensis,* a rare Chinese species, also turn from pearly white to softest rose.

The flowering crab, *Malus Niedzwetzkyana,* has large, cone-shaped deep purple fruits with a greyish bloom.

Crataegus Wattiana, one of the hawthorn tribe, has attractive bright yellow translucent berries.

Amongst the barberries are some very beautiful berries; *B. chitria* has berries nearly an inch long, purple, almost black, and covered with bloom. *B. Wilsonae* has exquisitely tinted coral berries; *B. pruinosa* has wands of beautiful blue-black berries thickly covered with mealy bloom.

Hedera chrysocarpa, the Italian Ivy, has decorative yellow berries, while for those who value form more than colour, the common Ivy which flowers on old walls and in hedges, has soft greenish grey berries, beautifully arranged, contrasting gently with its sombre green leaves.

HINTS ON APPLYING MANURES

Never apply manures to dry soil. Always water well first, and then hoe lightly.

Avoid any contact with foliage by either dry or diluted manures, or they will be scorched.

Always measure your manures carefully: two ounces means two ounces; a tablespoon is not at all a reliable measure. When using liquid manure in a water can, always keep stirring with a stick, otherwise the last pint may be much too strong.

A small channel made in the earth round the base of a plant is the best way of applying liquid manure, but do not let it be too near the roots – about three inches from them will be safe.

Apply dry manures through a pepper box, or dusting powder lid; this will ensure its being equally distributed. Then hoe or prick in very lightly.

BEDDING HINT

When using Geraniums for bedding out, plant them on their sides, at an angle of forty-five degrees. The side shoots bear the best flowers, and this method produces the finest flowers.

.   .   .

A lovely tree for August flowering is *Robinia Decaisneana.* Pink is an unusual colour for trees at this time, and the flowers are a beautiful rosy pink, like wistaria flowers, and are highly effective drooping amongst the delicate acacia foliage.

Another August bloomer seldom seen is *Aesculus parviflora*, a shrubby chestnut, which grows some eight feet high, and has quantities of very delightful white flowers.

SEASIDE PLANTS

Nearly all flowers dislike salt, particularly the clinging salt of the sea mist.

If after every such mist you hose your garden down, you will find that your flowers are grateful, and show their gratitude very plainly!

TOPIARY

Although I adore form in the plant world I cannot endure the tortures of topiary. Could the topiarist, having made the thicket into a ram, endow the beast with animal life it might be a feat to call for pride. But why take a simple honest bush of box or yew, and twist and torture it into a stag or a peacock or a stork?

I don't decry perversity unless it offends my eye, but to see a natural living bush having its own beauty of form, transformed into a monstrous beast or bird is indecent from a natural beauty point of view.

Had nature intended there should be Box Beasts or Yew Storks – animals with coats of leaves instead of fur, she would certainly have produced them. No topiarist can turn a peacock into a tree, thank Heaven.

There was, of course, that old, rather disgraceful business of turning Daphne into a laurel, but that was apparently a matter of deadly expediency. (Probably she was extremely annoyed to find her maidenly appeal heard, realizing that as a laurel she had no posterity!)

But the Box and the Yew have no such need of being transformed into an animal of any kind; no violent hand is laid upon the shrub but that of the topiarist.

The finished abortion looks neither an animal nor a shrub. It has but the clumsy outline of the former, the pinched and prisoned leaves of the latter. It produces those villainous adjectives, 'quaint', 'priceless', 'droll', and 'odd', which should never apply to the beautiful creatures of the plant world.

Many a gardener is too meddlesome with the knife. To get a few extra or out-size blooms, he often sacrifices the graceful shape of the tree. Let him remember the topiarist and pause!

WILLOW FENCING

An admirable 'hedging' for fields is the Willow. Willows do not, as trees, transplant well, and the best and cheapest thing to do is to take Mr. Bean's advice, and plant six foot 'rods' about the size of a thick walking stick, any time between November and February.

It is mistaken to suppose that Willows thrive only in moist situations. Many of them do equally well on agricultural land, though a few of them prefer chalk.

To keep the brilliant tints of the coloured barked Willows, which are intensely brilliant in the winter, the plants must be pruned hard every year in very early spring, preferably the end of February, as the colour is brightest upon the new year's shoots.

.   .   .

Above the black battalions of the trees,
Through troops of funeral cloud the gardener sees
The moon lying in state amongst her stars.

CLUMPS

Ugly word with beautiful usage. Too many gardeners are prone to 'sprinkle' their herbaceous borders with a miscellany of flowers. Here a Delphinium, here an Iris, here a Phlox, and here again a Poppy, a Lupin, a Paeony.

Many flowers are ill suited to such treatment: many look far better growing entirely alone, though this is not always possible, for questions of floor space. But certain plants could be grouped in clumps. Irises, if grown in the harbaceous border, should be so grown; their foliage, after the blooms have gone, makes a pleasant oasis of green. Lilies look much more effective grown in clumps; so do Gladiolus, and nearly all plants that do not themselves make a formidable clump.

The most sensitive colour scheme is needed to plant isolated flowers; they are far less likely to clash, when they are grown together, and thus maintain a solid mass of harmonious colour.

TEMPERAMENTAL PLANTS

Plants have habits and idiosyncrasies as evident and pronounced as those of human beings. They live their own lives within the confines of their existence, unperceived and unregarded by the casual beholder.

Because they do not shout nor grimace, nor use the undignified gestures of human kind, we consider them merely as the 'vegetable world'. But they have an existence, as complicated, as subtle as ours.

The Sunflower, for instance, does actually turn her head to follow the sun, and at dark turns that head back when she can no longer see him.

Mimosa pudica (the Sensitive Plant) closes its fragile leaves when touched or breathed upon. If a light, or a hot object is held near it, the leaflets snap together frantically, pair by pair, till shuddering, the whole leaf collapses from shock.

Lightly touch the floret of the hardy perennial, Dracocephalum, and it remains like a little signal at the angle to which you put it.

The grain of Mahogany, though maimed and tortured into furniture and veneer, still struggles undying towards the sun.

The beautiful tree, *Caesalpinia pluvosa*, is a 'weeper' in a very literal way. Tears pour continuously from its leaves, sometimes drop by drop, sometimes in streams, sun or shade, wet or fine. For some private sorrow, it just goes on weeping.

Sulphium lacinatum, a North American plant, sets it leaves so rigidly north and south that it makes a reliable compass.

Dictamnus Fraxinella surrounds itself with a cloud of volatile oil, which can be ignited with a match on warm, sultry evenings.

For some strange reason *Arnebia echoides*, a pleasant little annual, paints five dark purple spots on each primrose bloom, which fade away as the flower matures. Legend says that they represent the finger marks of Mahomet. Since Arnebia belongs to the Borage family and comes from Russia, she would probably give quite a different reason for the spots!

The Californian Pitcher Plant sets a snare of honey on her lips, and a bath of watery fluid in her breast for her luckless lovers, who cannot return from Paradise because of the fine downy hairs that bar the gates.

Aspen leaves tremble continually. On the mildest, stillest day they complain and whisper dolefully.

The seeds of the Mangrove remain fastened to the mother tree until they become young plants. Then they cut themselves from the fruit in which they have grown, and fall to the ground, and begin to grow for themselves.

The Broad Bean allows the humble bee alone access to her honey parlour!

TREES

The Cedar has no 'temperament'. The years have laid their might upon him. Centuries are in his branches. With the terrible, benevolent unconcern of God he stretches forth his arms, and there is thunder beneath them, and his breath is the incense of the Ark of the Covenant.

The Cedar belongs to none. The hand that planted it died centuries ago. No man can say 'My Cedar' any more than he can say 'My Mountain', or 'My Cathedral'.

Though we may inherit great trees, dare we say we possess things which we cannot hold, cannot move, cannot retain, cannot order, though we can, if we are vile at heart, cut down?

Some trees must be grown in groves to have beauty. A single Beech tree is not impressive, while a Silver Birch needs no company. A single Oak seems a timber torn from a ship; a single Elm betrays its uncouth outline. Yet a single Pine tree acquires an awful austerity. Its beauty is in its loneliness.

THE DAY LILY

In America Hemerocallis is highly regarded; here it is, with other choice plants, greatly neglected. It is a very old plant, known to many races. Pliny refers to it in his Natural History, and in Egypt it was known as Icroix.

It has useful medicinal properties, and in China is extensively used, both as food, medicine and flavouring.

Here, one seldom sees it in gardens, yet what a graceful good-tempered plant it is. It grows anywhere; sun or shade, clay or lime.

The plant makes a clump of shining sword-like leaves, from which spring long, slender but sturdy stalks, capped with lily flowers, azalea-like in texture; lemon and orange; and amongst the new hybrids, delicious shades of shell-pink and tawny red; and presents its daily bouquet for about six months in the summer, and the flowers are sweetly scented.

It is a lovely plant for the water garden, yet it adds a grace to the herbaceous border. The veriest amateur can grow it in any soil, yet it remains a stranger to the average gardener.

NURSERY FERNS

Amusing fern pots for the nursery may be made by children in the following manner:

Cut off three or four carrot tops, about an inch thick. Set them firmly on the tops of small jars filled to the brim with water. The carrots should fit neatly on the top like a lid. Trim them round if they are too big. Place these pots in a deepish bowl, and fill the spaces between with mould, so that the pots are hidden.

Put the whole thing in the dark, as you would bulbs, and when the carrots have sent roots down into the water, bring the bowl out, and place it on the window-sill.

Hide the earth and pot rims with shaggy moss, and very soon you will have a nice little pot full of carrot ferns!

LEAF MOULD

Oak leaves are the best of all leaves for making leaf mould; next comes the Beech leaf in value. The Poplar leaf is of no value; Sycamore and Chestnut do not decay satisfactorily, and both Ash and Elder leaves contain acids that are injurious to plants. These should all go into the garden bonfire.

.   .   .

Have you a shrub of *Olearia Haastii* in your garden? Cut it and place it in a blue or green jar. The sprays will dry slowly into a bunch of mellow brown seed heads, the leaves will blacken, and curl to show the underside of the leaf a pure silver white. Not a showy decoration, but of very quiet beauty.

THE ALPINE LAWN

M<small>R. CLARENCE ELLIOT, THE WELL-</small>known Alpine gardener, introduced this fascinating addition to the lovers of Alpine gardening.

To those who cannot afford the luxury of Westmorland stone or Tufa, it is a lovely boon.

The Alpine lawn is not a 'lawn' in the ordinary term. There is no grass, for grass would soon strangle the tiny Alpines.

It is entirely 'turfed' with dwarf 'creepers', and soon becomes a marvellous carpet of exquisite colour. Here and there flat stepping stones should be laid, for though one can walk on some of these tiny carpeters, it is a disgraceful thing to do.

The soil for this lawn must be deeply dug, and mixed with plenty of sand and leafmould. And then comes the planting, and after that, 'All's done with, watch who may, wait, and wear, and wonder who will'.

Get together, beg, borrow, buy or steal all manner of creeping Thymes, and Aceanas, Raoulia and *Mentha Requieni*, *Veronica Repens*, *Mazus rugosus*, and others.

Plant them six inches apart, and they will quietly, implacably, weave, plait, entwine themselves together into a flat, glowing tangle, waving small banners here and there triumphantly when special progress has been made in their engaging combat, humping together into little hills and crests, when they can creep no longer horizontally. The grey, green, gold, bronze, silver are spangled and starred here and there with colour. If you planted nothing else there your Lawn would be a dream.

But other lovely things can be grown here: the Anemones, *A. pulsatilla* and others, Gentians – if they happen to like it, some of them are faddy – the dwarf Campanulas; the nine-inch Potentilla with its cherry-red flowers; the Sisyrinchiums, the prostrate Veronicas, Fritillaries, Alpine Violas, the grey Festuca grass, Calamintha and small Heaths, and many other hardy Alpines.

Bulbs, too, can be planted here and there, though I don't like bulbs in a meadow, anyhow the sophisticated ones.

In some Alpine lawns, taller plants are permitted, but I think they spoil the effect, giving it too much of an herbaceous border illusion. Of course in the real Alpine meadows the plants run up to two feet, but they grow as thick as grass, making a kind of meadow 'level', which is very different from growing them in isolated groups above carpeters.

It is better to keep the level lower: occasional small outcrops of stone and dwarf shrubs will give the true heath appearance.

Never spoil the Alpine lawn by anything sophisticated, nor take to it anything from the garden border or bed, or the character of the Alpine lawn or meadow will be utterly spoiled.

The Alpine lawn may be an 'outcrop' of the larger rock garden, or it may form a centre, or opposite, to the smaller rock garden, or it may lie upon the lawn itself, provided that a suitable background is provided.

AROMATICS

How rarely we grow plants for their fragrance only. Some are foolishly apt to resent the space given to a plant which has little pretensions to colour or face beauty.

Many deeply fragrant plants have quite insignificant

blooms; Balm, for instance, many of the Thymes, most of the Mints. But the perfume they give is worth a hundred pink cheeks and blue eyes.

Rosemary has, I think, one of the most fascinating of perfumes, at once spicy and sweet. Its small, lavender flowers are inconspicuous, but brush it with your fingers in passing, and how rich a perfume lingers on your hand.

The upright variety, Miss Jekyll, is the best kind, from a decorative point of view, though the prostrate variety is more prettily flowered in purple. It is attractive sprawling over a warm flat boulder in a sheltered part of the rock garden.

Few of the Thymes have conspicuous flowers. *T. citriodorus argenteus* has silver-edged leaves and small lilac flowers; *T. serpyllum* has darker flowers; *T. carnosus* makes a little tree like a juniper, with small whitish flowers, but all have the rich, spicy family smell. *T. herba-barona* smells ravishingly of seed-cake.

T. membranaceus has, however, most beautiful large warm white flowers, and the varieties of *T. serpyllum*, *T. s.* Annie Hall and *T. s. coccineus* have quite gay little blooms, the former almost flesh-pink, the latter a splendid crimson.

Balm makes a pleasantly green clump of slightly harsh leaves of the most delicious lemon verbena perfume. Its flowers spoil it completely.

The Mints are strongly though not sweetly scented, except *Mentha rotundifolia*, which mixes pineapple with its native peppermint, and *Mentha Requieni*, one of the tiniest of all plants, who spreads a sweet carpet for the foot. Frankly, Pennyroyal (*M. pulegium*) is as vulgar in its smell as in its rampageous behaviour.

Artemesia Abrotanum is the beloved Lad's Love of old gardens, and its queer, pungent tang evokes a strong association of ideas: in childhood that grey, feathery Southernwood could be tracked in any garden.

Costmary, or Alecost, is seldom seen. It is tall, ragged, yellow, buttoned: no beauty, and smells of mint and some other vague spice of its own.

Rue has a very peculiar but rather pleasant smell, and is rather a decorative plant, with blue-grey leaves and heads of light yellow flowers. It makes a good little hedge for the kitchen garden.

The grey, woolly-leaved Sage conjures up the vision of goose, and is a comely-looking silver-grey bush.

You would not grow *Tussilago fragrans*, first cousin to the Coltsfoot, for the remarkable beauty of its flower!

It sends up cold, pale flowers, scarcely mauve, scarcely white, in a cluster on short thick stems. But this rather bedraggled person sends up these blooms in January, and the perfume of the flower is exquisite – filling a whole room with heavy fragrance. It does, I must admit, fill the whole garden with large leathery leaves if you allow it, for it is a spreader, a deadly spreader.

The shrub, Allspice (*Calycanthus floridus*) has very dull brownish-red flowers, but richly scented leaves and stem. I like the shrub, but a great many people would consider it plain.

Comptonia asplenifolia is a shrub very rarely seen, whose flowers are very 'off' white, almost a vague brown, but its beautiful fern-like leaves are very aromatic.

The flowers of the Cotton Lavender, *Santolina Chamaecyparissus*, are very plain, and are better destroyed at birth, but the plant itself is richly silver, and looks regal amongst darker shrubs, and has a lovely fresh scent.

The little Woodruff (*Asperula odorata*) has insignificant little whitish flowers, but the smell of its dried leaves brings back to us every hayfield we have ever tumbled in as children, and is worth growing for that alone.

The more beautiful the members of the Woodruff family are in looks, the less lovely do they smell.

Bergamot does not really belong to this story, because its flowers are beautiful – a deep, carnation red with not a trace of scarlet in them. But the plant sends forth its fragrance long before the flowers appear – an exquisite mixture of orange blossom and eau-de-Cologne in almost equal parts. And had it no perfume at all, it would still be a very handsome border flower.

.   .   .

When spacing and sowing seeds and plants, which need to be placed at equal distances, get a length of garden line, and make a knot at every six inches. This will ensure perfectly correct spacing.

THE QUIET GARDEN

Picture postcard gardens are lovely to look at – for a while, but most uninteresting to work in, and most exhausting to live in! All the jangle and scream of colour, the jumping red, the unquiet blue, the noisy yellow, tossed together like a skein of ravelled silks, to get that 'riot of colour' which is the Mecca of so many gardeners.

The vegetable garden is often a more pleasant place than the rowdy, crowded flower garden.

Give me the quiet green, with a glimpse of water; the soft colours of evergreens, flowers that are the part, not the whole of a scheme.

Give me, in short, a quiet garden, and you may take your bazaar of flowers.

HERBACEOUS BED

Why is the herbaceous border invariably placed length-wise in a garden? Because, you will murmur, length is the all in all of the herbaceous border! Yes, but length without breadth is a line, and that is what the usual herbaceous border becomes in the average narrow garden.

In the larger garden, the herbaceous border becomes a long wide swathe of colour, but this is impossible in the smaller garden, and since in a narrow garden, width at the side cannot be allowed, it is better to place the herbaceous border in another position.

And what better position than right across the garden? Here, although you cannot make it long, you can make it wide, and width seems to me far more important than length, since anyhow, you cannot get the vista effect that is part of the herbaceous border's charm in the larger garden.

The herbaceous border, which really becomes an herbaceous bed, gives a gorgeous effect from the house, and makes the garden seem twice as wide. Indeed, if you are flower crazy, you can have two herbaceous beds, separated by turf or crazy paving, pool or seat, flanked on either hand by glowing colour; or a wide herbaceous border beyond a broad paved terrace will look extremely effective, the turf leading up to the terrace, from the house. Such a bed will be very much easier to work, for you can tend it from both sides.

If you plan two herbaceous beds in such a position, you will, of course, plant your nearer one with shorter plants, and here and there a tall clump, leaving such things as Hollyhocks, Verbascum, and other giants to the second border, where you can get the effect of a flower fence.

Try this plan, and you will never again plant that 'ribbon' border along your fence, and be content to call it an 'herbaceous border'.

RED ROSE JAM

Gather a pound of red roses, and boil them lightly in two pints of water, keeping the lid on. When tender strain off the coloured juice, and leave on the stove while you add four pounds of castor sugar, one pound at a time, stirring well until it is thick and syrupy. To this add the petals, mix well, let it get cool, and pot down.

This jam is good mixed with sliced bananas and two tablespoons of orange juice, placed in sundae glasses topped with whipped cream.

.   .   .

Little muslin bags filled with dried Southernwood lightly broken up, hung in wardrobes and placed among furs, are a pleasant and effective remedy against moths.

CUT FLOWERS

To prevent the greenish slime which clings to the stalks of cut flowers, put a lump of charcoal in the water.

A penny placed at the bottom of the vase revives

flowers marvellously, particularly the long-stemmed florists' roses which so often wilt before the buds open.

Sweet Peas, Lilies, Pinks, Mignonette, dislike company in vases, and should not be mixed. Roses dislike the company of flowers with fat fleshy stems. (One can't blame them!)

Break or bruise an inch of the flower stalks before putting in the vase, so that they can take up more water; otherwise the sap will seal the end.

Cool air at night revives flowers that have been in a warm room all day, so place them in a cold room at night.

Flowers that last long in water are Helichrysums, Carnations, Chrysanthemums, Scabious, Heleniums, Alstroemerias, Pyrethrums, Gaillardia, Montbretia.

FENCES AND TRELLIS

When using trellis work to heighten a fence, do not fasten it to the fence itself, but to wooden uprights a few inches from the fence.

House walls covered with trellis work are often a problem. If the trellis is hinged at the bottom, and fastened at the top with brass hooks, it can be moved slightly forward for any necessary cleaning or repairs, without undue injury to the climber on it.

In building a new fence, always use reinforced concrete for the uprights. Even oak, which is usually used, will rot in heavy soils.

A cheap method of repairing rotting uprights is to fasten a T iron support to them. This ensures absolute rigidity, and is cheaper and more satisfactory than spurs.

Never pile earth against wooden fences higher than the skirting board, or the fence will soon rot. The skirting board itself is easily replaced. Never attach a washing line to a wooden fence: the strain is too great.

A fence belongs to the person to whom 'the nails are pointing' in building language; in simpler language, the side of the fence which bears the supports. It is well to remember this when buying a house.

SCHEMES FOR WINTER DECORATIONS

Flowers for winter decoration are always a problem – and an expense – but the true flower lover feels something is missing in a room without flowers. Of course, there is always the vase of Chrysanthemums to be had, the flowers from the florist – the ubiquitous bulb bowl, but there are various original decorative schemes which require only the minimum of flowers.

If you have a china figure of any kind, an animal, a nymph, a child or a cottage, for instance, it will look delightful placed in a round shallow bowl, filled with moss, starred with a few Violets, Anemones, Snowdrops, or a few flowering twigs of Hamamelis, or Winter Jasmin.

When the flowers have faded, they can be picked out, and other small flowers may take their place. This makes a perfect decorative table centre, and plaster figures of nymphs and children are so cheap that if you have none, it is well worth buying one or two.

If you are a lover of green, instead of the flowers, sprays of the lighter evergreens, such as the Cupressus, make a lovely 'forest' bowl.

Little bushes of Veronica, with their box-like leaves, will grow for a long time in water, if you renew it constantly. One placed in a light-coloured bowl with narrow neck makes a delightful little tree for your room.

Or cut some stout sprigs of Lavender, and fill your shallow bowl closely with them, letting your plaster figure rise from the centre, and place one or two Christmas Roses amongst the soft grey leaves.

A shallow bowl filled with moss and stuck over with Christmas Roses is a good way of using this flower, which is rather difficult from a vase point of view.

If you have a witch bowl, you can get a most original effect by putting your figure at the bottom of it, filling it with water, and covering the surface with brilliant, short-stalked flowers.

Another very delightful, though more artificial effect for tall jars or witch bowls is to fill them with sprays of Laurel leaves which have been painted all over with silver aluminium paint. They last for a long time, and give a wonderful effect of brightness.

The little Button Daisy, uprooted bodily from the garden, will grow gallantly planted in moss in a shallow bowl, and it will not be very long before they cover the bowl with their saucy, innocent faces. This is nice for a centre piece for the table.

A few branches from the deciduous shrubs in your garden, picked and arranged in a vase will, owing to the warmth of the room, not be long before they put forth tiny leaves of a delicious green. The Currant is one of the prettiest, and later on, will produce its flowers. Curiously enough, in the case of both yellow and pink flowered currants, the blooms indoors will be waxy white, though still retaining their characteristic spicy odour.

Other fancies are tiny woodland seedlings planted in damp fibre, covered with moss, and starred with anemones, the stalks of which have been cut short.

These suggestions should go far to give your rooms 'something different' in the way of decoration.

RELIEF FOR ROSES

A good remedy against rose mildew is 1 ounce of bi-carbonate of soda to 10 gallons of water, used as a spray.

BEE PLANTS

The following flowers are all particularly rich in nectar:

Nepeta, Cornflowers, Clover, Campanulas, Aubrietia,

Mignonette, Wallflowers, Hollyhocks, Scabious, *Arabis Alpina*, Limnanthes, Crocus, Forget-me-not, Thyme, Honeysuckle, *Sedum spectabile* (the Japanese Stonecrop), Michaelmas Daisies, Borage, Phacelia, Strawberries.

Amongst trees and shrubs, Ivy, Daphne, Box, Berberis, the Lime and Sycamore, Pear, Plum, Cherry and Apple trees, and the Raspberries and allied berries, Currants and Gooseberries, are all beloved by bees.

The early and late flowerers amongst these plants are of special value, because at these times pollen is difficult to obtain.

OTHER EDGINGS

One may tire, or one may not, of Mrs. Simpkins. One certainly tires of Lobelia and Calceolaria.

And there are many wholly delightful little borderers that should be given a trial.

One rather unconventional one is the Alpine Strawberry (*Fragaria*, Bush Alpine, Red). But it makes a very nice, compact, satisfactory edging; the flowers are quite pretty enough, and it fruits just as well in the front of a border as in the kitchen plot. It is not particular as to soil, and makes no runners, remaining a tidy little bush throughout the season.

The Alpine grass, Festuca, six inch, makes a very beautiful, though not a cheap edging, but its fine glaucous grey blades offer a splendid foil to any colour, and its growth is admirable.

The neglected, rejected, insulted London Pride is a favourite edging of mine. Most people, if they grow it at all, let it heave itself into large mounds, which are untidy for bordering. But if London Pride is not allowed to make its bed as it pleases, and is reduced to a tidy line of two or three rosettes, it is a delightful edger.

A quaint borderer, for those who like variegated plants, is *Arabis variegata*, whose leaves are green and custard colour. Like London Pride, *Arabis* must be kept within bounds, and since the flowers do not add to its beauty they should be removed at birth. Both this *Arabis* and *A. Billardieri*, which has grey leaves and not very pretty pink flowers, look far better polled and clipped into neat mounds.

Armeria maritima is a popular edging, but *A. mar. alba* is not so well known. It has white flowers, and makes an equally nice edging. It can be multiplied very easily by pulling rooted pieces from the old clumps in the autumn.

The little Campanula, *C. Portenschlagiana*, is another very pleasant edger. It is evergreen, some six inches high, and is prodigal of its dark blue flowers all through the summer. It can be divided without the least trouble.

White Button Daisies give an old-fashioned air to a not too lordly bed. I like them, for they are so neat and clean looking. Bride White is perhaps the best.

For an annual summer borderer, and if you like yellow, you cannot beat *Limnanthes Douglasii*, whom the bees love. It is not so tidy as some, but makes a beautiful wide swathe of large yellow, white-edged flowers, which blossom with tremendous profusion. It grows about six inches tall, and should be thinned out to six inches apart to get the best effect.

If you still hanker after Lobelia, get the white flowered kind. It makes a really dainty little edger, though it is not quite so floriferous as the old blue.

Veronica Teucrium dubia makes a pleasant borderer, too. Its compact leaf tufts are evergreen, and its pale wands of lightish blue are extremely graceful. It cares not where it grows, nor with what violence it is divided.

Corydalis lutea, the yellow fumitory, makes a graceful

borderer with its delicate ferny leaves and small yellow hooded flowers. Its early growth is particularly charming, and it does not give up the battle till repeated and persistent invasion by frost.

BIRD SCARER

Black cotton is a better bird scarer than any more expensive or elaborate contraption.

To protect rows of peas or other seedlings grown in rows, fix an iron garden hoop at each end. To one end tie an end of black cotton, and pass the cotton backwards and forwards, winding it round the hoops each time in lines from the ground up. Keep the thread taut.

The ends may be protected by passing the cotton across the hoop, so that the whole row is neatly covered with a cotton roof.

PODS

The seed vessels of many plants have a beauty of a very interesting and decorative kind. Few have the rich colours of the flowers from which they came, but in form and interest they must appeal to every gardener.

The Oriental Poppy pod has all the beauty of unpolished wood – with its carved filigree seed canister. The pods of *Dictamnus fraxinella* are three-pronged, and have a strong aromatic odour like a harsh lemon verbena. They open to disclose a pearly inner seed-chamber, which encloses small, piercingly black-china seeds.

Collutea, the Bladder Senna, has very decorative pods. At first they are soft green, veined with red, having the substance of kid blown out like small oblong balloons which, when squeezed emit, the air with a sharp report. Afterwards they become as hard as parchment, split, and let fall their seeds.

Broom pods are fascinating. Their soft green colour makes broom branches very effective for indoor decoration. As they mature they become black and wrinkled like kid gloves, finally withering and splitting when the sun forces them, and shooting their brown seeds with small explosions many feet across the garden.

There is no need to extol the beauty of the silver Honesty, nor the brilliant lanterns of Physalis, the Chinese Lantern. Many of the Roses bear vividly hued seed satchels. R. Moyesii has polished coral, beautfully shaped flagon pods, prickly and brilliantly coloured.

The tiny seed pods of Cynoglossum, though not

individually interesting, make quite a decorative spray. They are fastened to the under-side of the drooping stems, and are strongly burr-like in character. Probably in their wild state they grow thus so that they can transfer themselves to any small animal passing underneath.

The Cape Figwort has rich brown, rather hooked pods, useful for mixing with autumn flowers.

The Teazel Heads are not uncomely, with their large burr heads and stiff hooked bracts. The Teazel has the prized reputation of being irreplaceable by machinery in the 'combing' of various kinds of cloth.

The wild Yellow Rattle has prettily shaped, light brown pods, full of rattling seeds; the pods of the Bladder Campion are like small ochre tinted bladders.

One of the most decorative of pods in its earlier stages is that of Nigella (Love-in-the-Mist), which is an elegant melon-shaped capsule, crowned with spiny horns, and surrounded by the fine hairlike foliage of the plant. Dried carefully, they look well placed among immortelles in the winter.

The seed vessel of the wild Iris is very beautiful, as it ripens and displays its rows of bright orange vermilion teeth.

The pods of Nicandra (Apple of Peru) are very like those of Physalis, the berries being contained in a papery five-winged balloon.

VIBURNUM RHYTIDOPHYLLUM

The attractions of this remarkable Chinese shrub lie not in its umbels of white flowers, nor in its rich red berries. Without them the plant would be just as striking, for its beauty lies in its growth.

It is a strong grower, reaching about ten feet in height, with large dark green wrinkled leaves, the under sides densely covered with silver felt. The stems are covered with rich buff-coloured fur, and the leaf buds, also thickly felted, rise like curved horns all over the shrub, ending in small felted flower buds. These flower buds, which appear in autumn, remain unchanged all through the winter, flowering in May or June the next year. The contrast between the rich soft buff felt and the dark lustrous green is beautiful.

The shrub is quite hardy even in cold, bleak localities.

THE DARKER HELENIUMS

The old 'Sneeze Weed', the Helenium, is one of those plants that have been spoiled for us by seeing the old-fashioned rather glaring yellows in our childhood's garden. But some of the darker varieties now grown are truly magnificent.

H. Pelegrina, two and a half foot, is one of the darkest, its blooms a deep bronze mahogany. Crimson Beauty, eighteen inches, has brilliant red bronze flowers: *H. rubrum*, four foot, has large ruby chestnut flowers; Moerheim Beauty, three foot, has rich ruby variegated flowers, some three inches across.

The Heleniums are indispensable, both for the border and the vase; their hardiness and their season, August to October, make them doubly valuable.

These darker Heleniums are far more attractive than the bright yellow varieties, though there is a variety, William Marshall, whose flower colouring is salmon apricot, and because of its unusual colour, well worth including.

It is often argued against the Heleniums that their petals curve back so tightly that the flower looks only a ball. Half an ounce of sulphate of potash to one gallon of water will teach them better.

SHRUBBERY FLOWERS

People with the incurable itch for flowers in all parts of the garden can deck their shrubberies if they please.

It is a good thing for the shrubs, as it keeps the surface moist, and the flowers don't mind, for they are shallow rooters.

The yellow fumitory, *Corydalis lutea*, takes very kindly to the shrubbery, and makes delightful patches of fringed leaves and cheerful yellow flowers.

The small hardy Cyclamen nose happily amongst the tree roots. The Dog's Tooth Violet likes these quarters, the Foam Flower, *Tiarella cordifolia*, with fluffy spires of spiraea-like flowers grows rapidly among the shrubs, and so does *Tiarella unifoliata*, much more splendid in its cream plumes, about twelve inches tall.

The little Periwinkle has been almost overworked in such a position; one remembers the dreary little ramblers hanging over hideous brickwork beneath the drips of trees, but there is a white variety which banishes this doleful memory.

Wood Anemones do quite well here; so do Trilliums, though I should think it shameful to plant such beauties amongst the lower branches of shrubs!

Woodruff (*Asperula odorata*) knits its way busily about, here, and smells divinely.

The hardy kind of Tradescantia (*virginiana*) does not mind dense shade at all, and is very beautiful with its shining reed-like leaves of three-petalled flowers of blue, violet or white; but it wants moisture.

A good little carpeter-shrub is *Gaultheria procumbens*. It grows about four inches high, is glossy leaved with rosy white little flowers and red fruit. It does not, however, like lime.

Another excellent little shrub for the job is *Mahonia repens* – a miniature of the well-known *M. aquifolium*, but less than a foot high, making dense carpets, and even flourishing under conifers.

CAMPANULA THYRSOIDES

The lover of Campanulas will probably dislike *Campanula thyrsoides*. Those who do not care particularly for Campanulas will adore it.

It makes a rosette of narrow, downy leaves, from which spring a sturdy little blunt spire crowded with upturned tubular, palest lemon coloured bells, which give a delicious perfume. It grows some nine inches high, and is unfortunately a biennial, though easily raised from seed.

It has a queer charm, absent from many of the Campanulas.

ALPINE GARDEN

To a large number of gardeners, the Alpine garden in all its manifestations makes the greatest appeal.

'Rock Garden' has become so loose a term, and has so wide a boundary that it embraces flowers and shrubs that are not Alpine in character, but to the observant gardener there is a certain spiritual affinity between plants, and I feel that plants for the true Alpine garden should be neither large nor tall, nor in any way suggestive of the herbaceous border; that no border-line plant should be admitted there.

I would have no plant in the Alpine garden over a foot high. It seems a place for samplers and miniatures. The samplers may be on a large scale, but they should be flat like tapestry; the miniatures may repeat themselves, but they are still miniatures.

If an Alpine garden contains bold, tall things, it might just as well be a border, with the Alpines for carpeters. Stone, properly placed, small spires of dwarf tree or shrub will give all the height needed. The modern Alpine garden seems to have become very 'rock conscious'. There is a good deal of rock visible in the 'Show' gardens – when I say 'visible' I mean one is acutely conscious of the rock foundations beneath the trailers, cliff clingers, and rock huggers.

This 'building', successful in the hands of the experienced architect, is a snare to the beginner, and rock gardens have become a slave to stone, as borders have become a slave to colour.

'A little bit of stone, but good', is the safest slogan for the amateur. Stone is difficult to handle, and a ton or so of smallish pieces is apt to turn rock garden into quarry.

A few large, well-shaped stones, deeply sunk in the ground will be enough for the smaller rock garden. Since he can never hope to reproduce the authentic Alpine background, it should be the aim of the rock garden builder to make his as quiet and as unobtrusive as possible.

POISON FLOWERS

Many delightful and innocent-looking plants are murderers, however their appearance deceives one.

The poisons vary in degree, from the death-dealing dose of the tall Monkshood and Deadly Nightshade, to the slight skin poisoning produced by some of the primulas.

One might suspect Deadly Nightshade, with its livid flowers and black evil-eyed berries, of producing the deadly hyoscyamine and atropine, but who would suspect the lovely yellow-haired Laburnum of carrying a *porte monnaie* of deadly seeds?

Who would think that the wild Thorn Apple, with its frail white trumpets, hoards stramonium?

One might suspect the Poppy of a crime passionel; she hides beneath her crimson cape a packet of opium.

Monkshood or Aconite is altogether dangerous, leaf and root alike being poisonous.

The Hemlock (*Conium maculatum*) is another poisoner. Both the graceful feathery leaves and green berries contain conia, a few drops of which may prove fatal.

The Wild Hemlock, Water Dropwort, belonging to the same family, has intensely poisonous roots.

The Foxglove has a slightly mysterious air, with its discreetly lowered eyes, and contains digitalis, which is poisonous in large doses.

The beautiful Colchicum with her ethereal cups can

produce a powerful emetic which goes ill with her delicate looks.

The beautiful Lacquer Tree, *Rhus verniciflua*, contains sap which while being the base of Japanese lacquer, contains a violent skin irritant, while its brother, *R. toxicodendron*, should never be planted in the garden, as it is even more virulently poisonous.

One of the Ampelopsis family (*A. Hoggii*) gives severe skin inflammation: it may be distinguished from the harmless and popular Virginian creeper by its three leaflet leaves, instead of the five of the harmless creeper.

A plant of which one might suspect treachery is the Wild Arum. But while a taste of its juice burns the tongue and mouth for hours after, its roots produce a perfectly harmless, though somewhat uninteresting substitute for arrowroot.

The potato family has some very dangerous members in its family tree. Besides the Thorn Apple and the Deadly Nightshade, whose country name, Dwale, means 'mourning', the Henbane, a rather handsome, in a repulsive manner, wild flower, with large sticky leaves, and squat trumpets of dusky cream-coloured flowers, purple veined and dark eyed, brews a dangerous narcotic.

The leaves of the Nicotine, also belonging to this Borgia family, are violently poisonous if *eaten*.

Rossetti's Woodspurge has a cup of three, and its milk-white juice raises very painful skin blisters. In fact many members of the Euphorbia tribe are extremely dangerous in this way, including the Manchineel Tree, the Dog Mercury of woodlands, and the Manioc a plant from which the harmless tapioca are eventually evolved.

AUTUMNAL CLEAN

The tidy gardener who reduces his garden to a tidy level every autumn is dallying with many lives.

In Nature the dried stems and withered leaves stand above the plant, protecting it from frost, and from the winds that dry the roots. Very often the half-hidden heart of the plant is covered by a dense tangle of dried stems carried at some height from the plant; indeed the skeleton of the summer's plant keeps guard above the still living core of the next.

The Michaelmas Daisies are protected by their stiff, stout stems; the fern spreads a withered coverlet over the young fronds; many plants disappear entirely, leaving only a withered stalk as sentinel. Shrubs and evergreens strew their leaves about their roots.

It may be accepted as a rule, I think, that whatever guard is set over a plant by Nature should remain throughout the winter, for it is its natural protection.

Clearing away the fallen leaves from a bed may clear away slugs, but it clears away, too, some natural humus of the plant, and all its protection. Does not the mould-ered leaf help to provide food for next year, or why does it lie close round the plant when the year's work is over? In the wild, the plant must find its own nourishment, without help from manures and fertilizers.

The act of mulching is only an artifical protection for plants that are not grown naturally, and have thus lost the useful, food-giving litter about their roots. The plants that need this should be allowed to retain this natural food and shelter; plants that do not need it will not produce it.

Many Alpines make no preparation for the winter, because the snows of their natural haunts provide them with a deep, white blanket, which only melts when the surface is warm enough for the plants to start again. But when we grow them in our alien gardens, we have to give them artificial protection; the woolly Alpines are particularly repelled by our damp, rainy winters.

Whatever the appearance, I would not cut down a single stalk or stem till the worst of the frosts are over, and I would leave the leaf protection over tender plants later still. It is the penalty we have to pay for growing flowers where they were not born to grow!

THE TOAD LILIES

The Japanese Toad Lilies (*Tricyrtis*), like many other flowers, deserve more attention than they get.

Their only fault is that the flowers of some appear late in the Autumn, and are liable to be caught by the first frost.

But they are strange and curiously beautiful flowers, well worth the adventure.

T. Macropoda, twelve inches, is one of the most attractive, with white, starfish pointed flowers, heavily pocked with heliotrope, and an inner slender flower composed of anthers and stigmata, which are spotted with yellow and orange.

T. hirta is considerably taller, reaching four feet in height, its small white lily flowers spotted and stained with rose, seated in the leaf axil.

T. macrantha is a very lovely species. Its flowers are pure rich yellow, and much larger than those of *T. hirta* and *T. macropoda*. This species is rather more delicate too, demanding rich peaty soil and shelter.

There is a baby of the family that I have never seen, *T. nana*, just a few inches high, and hugging the ground, where it produces delightful yellow flowers. I believe this baby is delicate, and probably better in the Welfare Centre of the Alpine House!

The Japanese Toad Lilies like shade, but I have grown *T. macropoda* in loam and leaf mould, amongst boulders, facing east, and it flowers very well, though rather late, October usually.

FOR YOUR ADAM

The small gardener can make a charming little indoor garden very simply.

Cut off the tops of some beetroots and carrots, about half an inch thick, and trim the leaf stalks close. Then sit them on a plate. Put a little water in the plate (not enough to cover the stumps), and place on the window sill, keeping the 'roots' moist.

The bright green delicate fern fronds of the carrots will soon appear, while the beetroot will send up attractive leaves of yellow and rose.

FIRE LOGS

A log fire seems to bring the garden indoors. It conjures up the camp fire, and satisfies some primitive longing for the 'out-of-doors' that besieges the garden worker.

Oak makes one of the best fires, for it burns slowly and solidly for a long time, but it should be allowed to mature. Elm logs are poor fire makers; they burn quickly and somewhat sulkily. The chestnut when matured sends out very fierce heat, and birch and beech burn briskly but they should be stored for some months first. Ash burns well, green or grey.

Apple and pear wood are gay burners, and hiss pleasantly, giving out a pleasant odour.

Pine cones give out an intense, quick heat, and are wonderful for reviving an almost dead fire. Ships' logs burn very slowly, and the tar in them makes very beautiful blue and green flames.

BABY BRAMBLES

Two midgets of the ornamental raspberry family are: *Rubus articus,* which makes tiny clumps of erect stems, which support quite large bright rosy flowers for a long time in the summer. It makes a most obliging carpeter for bulbs in a cool, shady spot.

The other midget, *Rubus parvis* is even prettier. It makes a delicious small rock-garden shrub, and has large, papery white flowers.

A sunny corner, and loose, stony soil are its requirements.

A WHITE BUDDLEIA

One seldom comes across the Chinese *Buddleia Fallowiana alba.* Yet its long, thrusting spikes of white flowers with their bright orange 'eyes' are highly decorative. It has a rich, sweet scent, and the foliage is heavily silvered. A lovely shrub for a warm garden.

WHITE ANNUALS

COLOUR IS AS MUCH PRIZED AMONGST annuals as among perennials; consequently many attractive white annuals are neglected.

Nothing makes a better contrast to evergreens, and the cool whiteness soothes the glare of the herbaceous border.

For edgings, white or cream is the most satisfactory colour, since it jars with nothing in the bed, and beds of white flowers on the lawn are tranquil through hot summer days.

There is a very delicate white Nigella, for instance, which is extremely dainty amongst its fine green foliage, though it has the faintest blue tinge.

The annual Datura, *D. stramonium*, found growing wild on rubbish heaps, is an extraordinarily decorative annual for the herbaceous border. It has heart-shaped leaves, big, ivory trumpet flowers, and spined fruit not unlike the horse chestnut. You will find it in very few gardens, nevertheless.

The little white Lobelia has a charm totally lacking in its vulgar little blue brother, and makes a pleasant edging. White Nemophila is, I think, more interesting than the blue variety.

The white Wallflower is almost entirely forgotten amongst its lively brothers, yet its long spikes of rich ivory have an individual charm. It must not be planted with other Wallflowers though; the contrast is too violent.

Beside the blatant purple and washy pink of the Canterbury Bell, the white variety is an aristocrat. Double or single, or cup-and-saucer, the white Canterbury Bell deserves a choice spot in the herbaceous border, to which the coloured varieties should not aspire.

I never liked Ageratum, but the white variety, with its soft fluffy white heads, is quite a pleasant borderer, while the magenta Agrostemma has a delicate white sister who looks charming amongst her grey leaves.

Omphaloides linifolia is a lovely annual. Its leaves are silver grey, its large flowers are like ivory white Forget-me-nots. It grows a foot high, has a long flowering season – June to August – is excellent for cutting, and very little known.

How many gardeners grow white Poppies? Yet a line

of the large, double, deeply fringed silky White Swan variety, two feet, beats its scarlet brother hollow.

The big, double, white, quilled Zinnia, and the dwarf borderer Zinnia look like beautiful wax modelling and are exquisite against turf or evergreens.

There is a very nice variety of Sweet Sultan, which is delicately feathered in white. The flowers are large, on long stems, and sweetly scented.

The white Godetia makes a fifteen-inch bush, massed with pearly flowers, reminding one of a Cistus. The white Scabious has large pincushion heads of beautiful ivory, opening to feathery white.

One of the loveliest of the Viscarias is a dazzling pearly white, which looks delightful in large clumps.

I don't care much for the white Sweet William, but white Verbena is a very nice bedder, and the white Petunia, satin skinned and deeply fringed, is much more desirable than the coloured varieties.

You can have a lovely 'off-white' annual Lupin – a bed of these is charming; while the old, beloved Larkspur has a very fine stock-flowered, or single tall branching variety, which reminds one of Nigella.

The white Pentstemon too, with its drooping white bells, is lovely for cutting.

A very beautiful Evening Primrose is *Oenothera trichocalyx* (twelve foot) with silver leaves and large white papery flowers.

It is high time that the white annuals took a more prominent place in spring planting.

IMMORTELLES

The Helichrysums are usually thought of as flowers to be grown solely for winter decoration, but planted in groups in a sunny border they make very attractive tall clumps.

Give them good soil, to which plenty of manure has been added, to get really big blooms, and grow them in groups of one colour, bronze, amber and salmon.

They are excellent for cutting, lasting in water for weeks.

When drying for winter posies, the dried buds will open slowly if placed before a fire for a few moments. It is very curious to see the buds unfolding rapidly in the heat. They can be arrested in the state of unfolding at any moment, by removing from the heat.

THE SISYRINCHIUMS

How seldom one finds this family in gardens. One of the reasons may be that the naming of the plants is still in a state of confusion and argument, and certainly several with different names are indistinguishable.

But there are many delicately beautiful ones which deserve wider recognition.

One of the most beautiful is *S. grandiflorum*, with narrow grassy leaves and solitary flowers exactly like a snowdrop, except that the colour is a brilliant red-purple. This beautiful flower blooms in early February, and is perfectly hardy in well-drained soil and a sheltered nook. It dies down completely after flowering, so mark it with a cross!

Another exquisite one is *S. filifolium*, with the same narrow grassy leaves; on six-inch thinnest stems hang in June three or four snowdrops flower, veined delicately with violet, and very fragrant.

Amongst the taller members is *S. odoratissimum*, about eighteen inches high, with richly scented long deep yellow flowers like miniature lilies. *S. bermudianum*, which makes large clumps of very fine glaucous grassy leaves above which break sheaths of brilliant pure violet, starry flowers with golden eyes, a real beauty, disliking dry or chalky soil. It flowers from May intermittently to October, but only in sunshine.

S. striatum, about two foot tall, has flowers not unlike the flowers of a small mullein, pale yellow, neatly striped with brown and mauve, and delicate iris leaves. It likes cool soil, and since it is apt to deteriorate, it should be divided every year.

S. longifolium, a moisture lover, also listed as *Marica longifolia*, is a lovely plant, twelve inches, with large light blue flowers.

All the Sisyrinchiums like cool soil and moisture, and though they are said to resent disturbance, *S. bermudianum*, like *S. striatum*, does not object to it in the least, and each piece pulled away from the parent plant, very shortly becomes a large clump.

DELILAHS

Among the sorceresses of the plant world comes stealthy Nepenthe with death in her cup. The tall slender flagons have hinged lids which open to show delicate teeth. To lure her victims she paints her flagons with wicked violent colours, and places water at the bottom of them (some Nepenthes will hold nearly half a pint of water).

She sprinkles the tip of the pitcher with a few drops of glistening honey, and in go the luckless lovers – insects greedy for the love potion.

But before they taste of it, they find themselves sliding down the smooth pitcher sides, to be drowned in the water below.

In other varieties the pitcher looks like some devilish fishing line. The leafy lip lets down a kind of long rod, on the end of which is hooked a wondrous pot, half vase, half fish.

Others are fantastically spined; some dangle satchel-looking pouches. Many are brilliantly and extravagantly marked. All spell death in some guise.

.   .   .

So few things are wrong, so many stupid. Is it better to 'fling away ambition', and grow easy, pretty plants, or to waste time and money over plants that one is too ignorant to handle?

Is it better to succeed with Aubrietia, or fail with *Eritrichium nanum*?

FOR THE TREE LOVER

I find in myself a preference, almost unconscious, for plants that resemble trees, however remotely. The woody stem, the gnarled branch, however tiny, turns my heart from the delicate, soft growing herbaceous plants. I admire the creature that resists delicately the weight of air, that is not easily persuaded of the wind on her wanton journey, that is stubborned against heavy rain.

Colour is fleeting. Rain dishevels it: sun fades it. The little petal is easily tattered, the frost gags the delicate cup with silver. But snatch every stitch from a tree, and it is still noble, lithe, comely. Its most beautiful time is when the birds cry 'Spring!' in its naked branches, and the tiny nipples of green prick from the stirred wood.

CALLICARPA

Callicarpa Giraldiana is an unusual and decorative deciduous shrub. Its greatest beauty lies in its beautiful berries, which are round, and about the size of privet berries, but in colour a pure soft heliotrope. The berries are not glossy, but look as if painted with aluminium paint. Long after the leaves have fallen, these berries adorn the bare branches.

The shrub grows prettily, and to add to its beauties, possesses soft small rosy flowers, and an autumn leaf colouring of purplish rose.

'TENDER'

'Tender' is a treacherous adjective, applied to flowers, and often the gardener is aghast at its vagaries. For in colder gardens half-hardy plants survive, while in warmer gardens they are often killed by frost.

But so much depends on moisture. Plants in cold damp soils are more susceptible to frost than those in light, dry ones, even though they may have greater shelter.

I have observed an example of this in two gardens. One was perched high on the Wiltshire downs, the other lay in a comparatively sheltered garden, west of London. In the Wiltshire garden a shrub border was planted, facing west, backed by a wattle fence from the east, but exposed to the prevailing west and north-west gales.

In this border varieties of Cistus were planted: *C. purpureus*, *C. ladaniferus*, *C. salvifolius*; *Ozomanthus rosmarinifolius*, *Styrax japonica*, *Cestrum elegans*, *Olearia albida*, and other semi-hardy shrubs, usually marked 'tender' in nursery lists.

The same shrubs were planted in the other garden, in a border facing south, backed by a wooden fence, protected from the east. Yet in spite of the more 'favourable position', much to the owner's chagrin, the shrubs here were severely injured by frost during a winter when the shrubs in the more exposed garden escaped.

But there was one difference between the two borders. The Wiltshire border was a *raised border* on a slight slope, the other was perfectly flat, indeed slightly below turf level.

And that difference seemed to make all the difference! Cold air sinks, and finds the lowest level, as it undoubtedly found it in the 'sheltered hollow' border, while the r aised bed, being some six inches higher at least, escaped because the cold air sought a lower level.

This lesson seems to teach us that a raised bed or mound will help us to grow half-hardy shrubs in a less sheltered garden. Bracken or straw placed round plants acts in the same way, though the coverings placed round the shrubs in that more sheltered garden had no effect.

Yet many gardeners would have hesitated to plant those 'tender' shrubs in that bleak garden, and would have considered the 'warm South border' an ideal spot.

RESENTMENT

There are flowers which resent disturbance. They have builded great beauty, compact, fragile, complicated; taking months, perhaps years of secret labour to produce their finished work of art. Why should they not resent being torn limb from limb between the prongs of forks, or being wrenched out like a drawn tooth? Butchered to make a gardener's holiday?

They resent disturbance. I do.

·　　·　　·

People who 'love flowers' without any discrimination are as tiresome as people who 'like everybody'. No one of character can do either.

GARDENING AT THE WEEK-END COTTAGE

How OFTEN I HAVE HEARD THE apologetic, 'I'm afraid the garden's frightfully untidy, but I'm only here at the week-ends!' from the owners of country cottages.

The cottage owner who can afford a gardener has no such excuse to make, but there are heaps of week-enders who have to depend on themselves as gardeners, and do not know how to face the problem.

Week-ends are not enough to keep the ordinary garden either in repair or in beauty, particularly when the owner has guests to entertain, or visits to pay during the week-end. It involves an enormous spurt of energy, and not an hour for week-end loitering and leisure. And in many cases not every week-end can be spent at the cottage.

Nothing is more dismal than to bring friends down for the week-end and to open the garden gate upon disarray and neglect.

But with thought and by careful choice of tidy plants the week-end cottage garden can be both easy and beautiful. A sundial, bird bath or garden seat on a paved court, a trough garden on a small lawn, give more grace and character to a garden than the same space devoted to untidy borders.

The big herbaceous border should be forsworn, lamentable as that seems. But order is more essential than colour. The herbaceous border needs a lot of hoeing, weeding, staking, tying and the like, and since it occupies an important position in the garden its neglect is all the more apparent. It is far easier to keep small beds filled and tidy than one big one.

Too much grass is another snag. Either you spend hours mowing, rolling, edging and sweeping, or it looks like the field that the locusts haven't eaten! A hedge needs constant clipping and tidying; a gravel path needs a lot of weeding and rolling. In fact, the saviours of such a garden are stone, trees, shrubs and rock plants.

Take the first. All paths should be of cement or paving, home-made or otherwise, and part of the garden should be paved for sitting out, and to save labour. Crevices in the paving can be pleasantly filled with such things as Thyme, dwarf Veronica, Sedum, silvery Saxifrage, dwarf Campanula, Arenaria, dwarf Dianthus, dwarf Gypsophila and many others. Trim in the winter, gay in summer, these little plants are labour-savers, and yet make delightful pools of colour.

On the paved terrace, or piazza, larger spaces of any shape can be left for bigger plants. Dwarf Irises do perfectly well here, and are exquisite; Viola, Pulmonaria, Alpine Phlox, and bulbs in the spring all make concentrated groups of colour.

At the boundaries, particularly the north border, trees should be planted. No garden is a real garden without trees. Not Poplar, Chestnut, Lime or other trees with big leaves too heavy for the autumn sweeping, but Silver Birch, the tree without a peer. Its foliage is small, its shade light, its form graceful, its bark beautiful, and its leaves are easily swept back on the ground beneath it.

Other trees with light foliage and light shade for specimen or lawn trees are found among the beautifully coloured, small-leaved Japanese Maples, the Liquidambar, flame-coloured in the autumn; some of the new and beautiful Mountain Ashes; Gleditschia (the Honey Locust), whose leaves are like ferns; Halesia (the Snowdrop tree), the Robinia and weeping Birch, are all light and graceful.

Shrubs are perhaps the greatest boon of all. They have all the advantages, and none of the disadvantages of the larger plants. There are flowering shrubs for practically every month of the year, many of them out-rivalling the loveliest herbaceous plant. Do not forget, among them, the enduring evergreens, for these will give form and colour all the year round.

The varieties of Cupressus are invaluable; their foliage, palest grey-green, brilliant emerald, richest bronze or warm gold, will give you brightness long after the last flower.

For hedges that do not need the constant shears, choose *Thuya plicata*, *Cupressus Lawsoniana*, *Lonicera nitida*, or the *Laurel rotundifolia*. These make graceful hedges of a pleasantly informal kind.

Grey-leaved shrubs should be planted to blend with the grey of stone paths and walls. A hedge of Lavender requires very little attention, and the Cotton Lavender (Santolina) and silvery *Senecio Greyii* are also worth considering.

There is no need for only one rock garden. The rock garden can be a rock border or bank of any length, or several small ones can be placed in effective situations. And the advantages of the rock garden are precisely the same as those of stone, shrubs and trees – order with beauty.

Something is always going on in the rock garden, but there is no staking, tying, digging or hoeing once the garden is established.

And at long last, there are always Roses, the most obedient and considerate of flowers. These can be planted in separate colours in small borders that are easy to tend. Climbing Roses on a rough, open spruce fence make a lovely hedge, too. Hardy annuals, from seed, may be included, and some of the summer bedding plants.

In this way the week-end cottage garden will always be neat and gay, and still there will always be something to do – small, pleasant jobs that do not devour every hour of the precious week-end.

SUN DIAL

Life's sunny hours I tell –
All's well.
Life's shadows I tell none . . .
All's done.

THE POND CYPRUS

Taxodium distichum is a leaf-losing conifer of the very greatest charm. Its foliage, pale greeen in spring, changes to the richest rusty gold in the autumn.

When young it has a poplar-like growth, and makes a beautiful specimen tree on the lawn, where it is quite happy, though it grows more quickly near water.

It is intensely decorative, both in form and colour; *T. ascendens nutans*, a weeping variety of *T. distichum*, having lovely pendulous branches and close-clinging leaves.

TREES IN SPRING

The trees were most busily embroidering their summer gear, standing naked and unconcerned at their stitching.

There is no sight in the world more lovely than a naked tree dressing itself on a spring morning.

Compared with this all other nakedness seems uncouth and over emphasized. There is nothing but the spirit of disembodied joy in one's vision of the tree.

We do not see ourselves when gazing in this mirror.

STAR AND STRIPE

Two pretty spring bulbs are *Triteleia uniflora,* the Spring Star Flower, and *Puschkinia scilloides,* the striped Squill.

Star Flower is white, growing on a delicate stem of five or six inches; the star faintly suffused with blue, and has a sweet scent.

Striped Squill is blue, four inches high, with a darker vein on each little petal.

Both are easy to grow, Star Flower beginning to bloom in March, Striped Squill in April. Both should be planted in autumn.

They belong to that cheerful class of small flowers which are not beautiful, but of an appealing prettiness.

BONDAGE OF COLOUR

How often one hears, 'What a glorious bit of colour!' How rarely, 'What an interesting plant!'

In spite of the pioneers, the men who go exploring the

gardens of the world for new and interesting plants, how many discoveries are allowed to languish in nursery gardens, only kept in existence by the patience and enthusiasm of some true gardeners.

'Too little seen in gardens', is the pathetic tag that makes its small advertisement in vain. Save us from this bondage to colour!

Have you ever been conducted round the beautifully furnished, beautifully kept garden, which has about as much interest as a plate of boiled rice? There are the Asters, the Hollyhocks, the Canterbury Bells, the Stocks: there, in the rock garden is London Pride, and Alyssum, and Aubrietia, and baby Campanulas, and the commonest of the Saxifrages – every name you knew before you mastered your spelling primer!

Did you learn anything? You learned nothing. Yet all gardens should be able to teach something to the visiting gardener. Such gardens help nurserymen to live, but not to aspire.

All art is experiment. The garden is our canvas. On it let us paint something that is not just a copy of the Old Masters.

DELPHINIUM IMMORTELLE

Delphiniums may be 'immortalized' in the following way, an old cottage woman told me once.

Get a quart milk bottle, and fill three-quarters of it with water. Cut two or three of the blooms, when the lower part of the stem is in flower; strip the leaves from the lower part of the stem, and put the spikes in the water.

They must then be placed in a North room for ten days or a fortnight, and left there until they have absorbed every drop of the water, and have become quite dry.

From then they may be treated as an Immortelle – placed in a *dry* vase, where they will keep colour all the winter.

THE HUNGRY PRIVET

No plants should be placed near a privet hedge. It is one of the greediest of plants, and takes up a very large amount of nourishment from the ground near it.

If flowers have to be planted in this situation, sink a strip of corrugated iron vertically along the privet roots to prevent them extending in that direction. Flowers may safely be planted close to the hedge if this is done.

PHLOX FAILURE

It is not generally known that Phloxes often fail from lack of moisture. They are very partial to leaf mould, and a couple of inches of this round the roots, spread out about nine inches, will greatly help them.

.   .   .

We buy new books, new clothes, go to new places, see new plays, but too often we stagnate in our garden!

ALPINE STRAWBERRIES

For the little garden the little strawberry. Those who have small space, and less time than must be given to the

207

strawberry bed, should grow instead the Alpine strawberry.

True they will not get the same monstrous berries, but they are rich and juicy and amazing croppers.

As Alpine strawberries obligingly carry the berries above the leaves, no straw is needed, and as birds do not fancy them no nets are required. They make delightful kitchen borderers, and delicious jam. What more could you ask?

Bush Alpine red is the best; it makes neat clumps, which begin to fruit in July, and continue till early October.

DEVILLED COB NUTS

Fry the kernels a light brown in butter, keeping them on the move in the frying pan. When the tint you like, drain them on blotting paper. After which roll them very lightly in pepper, or salt.

GOLDEN TREE POPPY

If you have a sheltered wall, hasten to possess *Dendromecon rigidum*, the lovely California Tree Poppy. A tall slender thing, it grows some six foot tall; its narrow leaves are beautiful blue-green, its large beautifully shaped yellow flowers are strongly perfumed. It is indeed a Queen among poppies, and happy in poor ground and old mortar rubble. And in late September you will still find it in flower.

ROAMERS AND RUN-A-BOUTS

I once asked an exhibitor why he had no *Clematis tangutica* amongst the Clematis he was showing.

'We've some lovely plants in the nursery,' he answered, 'but people only seem to want what everyone else has.'

Yet surely half the charm of a garden is the 'something new'? We should get very tired of shop windows that showed the same things all the time, and this applies to gardens.

There are, for instance, lovely climbers which are quite as attractive as the Rambler Roses, yet a hundred Dorothy Perkins are bought for one *Clematis tangutica*, or *Celastrus articulatus* or *Hydrangea petiolaris*.

This Japanese Hydrangea is a climber. It is hardy, climbing like ivy by aerial roots, and bearing large heads of thick-textured ivory flowers. In full flower, against a sunny wall, in July, it is delightful.

Celastrus articulatus is another climber not nearly so well known as it should be, possibly because its greenish flowers are not at all showy. But it atones for these in the autumn when its twining branches are laden with yellow, bead-like fruits which burst and disclose dazzling scarlet seeds.

I think *Clianthus puniceus*, the New Zealand Lobster Claw, would be more grown were it not undoubtedly tender. This means a sunny or warm wall in a sheltered garden. But should you have this very sheltered garden, everyone will envy you its possession. It grows elegantly and its brilliantly red flowers are like a lobster's claw.

Aristolochia sipho (Dutchman's Pipe) is, on the other hand, a hardy fellow, neither brilliant nor beautiful, but it's the kind of plant that makes visitors exclaim, 'Whatever's that?' when they see the queer purplish-yellow, pipe-like flowers.

I am very fond of *Clematis tangutica* with its yellow Chinese lantern bells on long black hatpins, which turn to tousled heads in late October. The Grace Darling Clematis, brilliant carmine rose, and Duchess of Edinburgh, compact, double, scented, very like a white camellia, and *Clematis cirrhosa*, with greenish white flowers that perfume the air in February, are others that appeal strongly to me.

Some of the variegated Ivies deserve more attention. *H. rhombea variegata* is highly decorative, with leaves boldly margined in white and *Hedera dentata aurea* with almost golden leaves.

The exquisite *Tropaeolum speciosum* or Flame Flower is hardy, though some people find it difficult. While it likes its head in the sun, it hates sun on its feet. Plant the long white tubers horizontally, four inches deep, in a wide hole of leaf mould on the shady side of a hedge, and it will wander round to the sun. People who can't grow this lovely creeper in leaf mould or anything else are advised to thump it into heavy clay. Some gardeners grow it easily like this, and swear that it is the only way!

A really lovely climber is *Schizandra grandiflora*

rubriflora, a strong grower, and best left to tangle round a pole or arch. Its flowers are ruby-red, in long spikes among thick shining leaves, and if you plant both male and female forms you will get bright fruits on the red-stemmed branches! It only dislikes really cold districts.

The blue Passion Flower, *Passiflora coerulea*, is seldom grown out of doors, but it is a charming plant for a warm, sunny wall. It flowers freely from June to September and is fragrant.

Annual climbers are indispensable for new arches or trellis, and I give pride of place to *Cobaea scandens*. If bought in a small pot and planted out in May, in an incredibly short time it will cover an arch with innumerable tendrils and produce large green cup-and-saucer flowers, streaked with purple.

There is no need for walls to go bare with all these lovely run-a-bouts from which to choose. And what can feed the pride of a gardener more than to hear a visitor exclaim, 'What a lovely thing! I've never seen it before!'

INTERESTING PLANTS FOR THE
ADVENTUROUS GARDENER

R. *alpines*   H. *herbaceous*   S. *shrubs*
C. *climbers*   W. *woodland*   T. *trees*

R. *Erythronium californicum* White Beauty 6 in. An exquisite Dog's-Tooth violet. Not in the least like a violet, but resembles an ivory white Turk's Head lily with white stamens. Partial shade, moisture, good drainage.

R. *Iris danfordiae.* A 3 in. beauty supporting on a slender leafless stem a brilliant little golden iris. Rich, well-drained soil.

W. *Ornithogalum nutans.* 1 ft. spires of paper-white drooping lily flowers, the outside of the petals translucent green with white edge. A most lovely thing, thriving in partial or dense shade. Good for cutting.

H. *Morina longifolia.* 2 ft. An old-fashioned flower, handsome and sturdy. Decorative thistle leaves, and substantial spires of drooping bells, first white, then flushing to pink, and so to deeper rose, the three colours on the plant at the same time. Rarely seen, but why not? Any soil, sun.

T. *Prunus pissardi nigra.* Pale beetroot buds gleaming on long thin black stems, and purple leaves. An elegant little tree for any soil.

H. *Daffodil Beersheba.* Well named! An enormous pure white daffodil waking covetousness! Not a speck of colour anywhere. The best white daffodil grown.

R. *Rhodohypoxis platypetala.* Compact mound of close foliage holding almost stemless ivory flowers of thick texture, star shaped, eyeless. Rare and delicious. A connoisseur's plant. Sun and sandy soil.

S. *Stachyurus praecox.* 6 ft. (about). A beautiful red-stemmed shrub with racemes of effective pale yellow bead-like flowers on leafless branches in late February. Hardy. Not nearly well enough known.

H. *Ostrowskia magnifica.* 3 ft. Glorious but touchy Campanula. Immense wide saucers of shimmering lilac silver. Small roots imperative, as any damage to the very long fragile root is highly resented. Very deep, good soil, and a sunny wall.

R. *Symphyandra pendula.* Exquisite tumbling over a rock in spate of large translucent bells of yellow green in August. Rich deep soil.

R. *Iris bucharica.* 1 ft. From bright pale green enfolding leaves come satin white standards and chrome yellow falls. Sun. Well-drained soil, a little lime rubble.

H. *Gladiolus tristis.* $2\frac{1}{2}$ ft. Very slender, delicate stems with sweetly scented pearly flowers stained with softest green. Lovely for cutting. Plant November. Well-drained soil, 4 in. deep. Protect with straw through winter.

R. *Satureia montana illyrica.* 6 in. A jewel for the rock garden in late summer. Little aromatic bushes loaded with violet flowers in August and September. Sun, sandy soil. Not a great beauty, but pleasant companion.

C. *Vitis vinifera purpurea.* Gorgeous foliage of rich ruby claret and richer purple. Leaves well shaped and not too large. Glorious colour against evergreens.

S. *Ribes speciosum*. A quite 'other' currant. The low bushes are hung with long brilliant scarlet fuchsia-like flowers. A very lovely shrub on any soil.

H. *Dicentra glauca*. Rare species of the old garden favourite, 'Bleeding Heart'. Makes a graceful bush of glaucous leaves hung with cream-coloured, rose-tipped 'hearts'. Most lovely. Leaf mould, sandy loam and sun.

T. *Salix Boydii*. A tiny tree, and very expensive if one goes by size! Six inches of venerable stumps, gnarled and stout, covered with little sage-green leaves. Looks about 100 years old. Only a connoisseur's tree.

– . *Cornus Natalii*. A very handsome cornel indeed. It has large ivory-green flowers, filled with a bunch of greenish stamens, rather like a clematis in shape.

T. *Populus candicans*. A scented poplar which gives out from bursting buds in springtime a most delicious aromatic odour, scenting the air for a long distance.

R. *Anemone sulphurea*. 12 in. An exquisite anemone like a rich lemon-yellow A. *pulsatilla*. Shade. Loam, a little grit, and leaf mould.

S. *Cytisus purpureus.* A small compact bush covered with rosy purple pea flowers. A very delightful dwarf broom. Any good soil and sun.

S. *Lonicera syringantha.* 6 ft. Slender, spreading shrub, glaucous leaves and lilac-pink flowers in May, and smells like lilac. The stems make delicate arches of bloom.

W. *Phytolacca aginosa.* 5 ft. Broad dock leaves, and chestnut spikes of round pink buds opening out into tiny May flowers. Large bright black berries follow. Handsome for the woodland garden. Dislikes disturbance.

C. *Schizandra chinensis.* Lovely twiner for deep loam, with beautiful large deep rose flowers in May, and long spikes of scarlet berries. Rarely seen, but certainly should be.

INDEX

INDEX

221

If you have enjoyed this Persephone book why not telephone or write to us for a free copy of the Persephone Catalogue and the current Persephone Quarterly? All Persephone books ordered from us cost £10 or three for £27 plus £2 postage per book.

PERSEPHONE BOOKS LTD
59 Lamb's Conduit Street
London WC1N 3NB

Telephone: 020 7242 9292
Fax: 020 7242 9272
sales@persephonebooks.co.uk
www.persephonebooks.co.uk